To Gordon

Best Wishes

From

All at Weston Ambulance

Station.

THE SAVE & PROSPER BOOK OF

ENGLAND'S
GRAND SLAM
1991

Rob Andrew
and
Dean Richards

with
Ian Robertson and Mick Cleary

STANLEY PAUL
London Sydney Auckland Johannesburg

Stanley Paul & Co Ltd

An imprint of Random Century
Random Century House
20 Vauxhall Bridge Road
London SW1V 2SA

Random Century Australia (Pty) Ltd
20 Alfred Street, Milsons Point, Sydney 2061, N.S.W.
Random Century New Zealand Ltd
PO Box 40-086, Glenfield, Auckland 10
Century Hutchinson South Africa (Pty) Ltd
PO Box 337, Bergvlei 2012, South Africa

First published 1991

ISBN 0 09 175173 X

Produced by Lennard Books
a division of Lennard Associates Ltd
Mackerye End, Harpenden, Hertfordshire AL5 5DR

Photographs by All Sport Photographic and Mike Brett
Design by Cooper Wilson
Colour origination by Amega Litho
Printed and bound in Great Britain by
Butler and Tanner, Frome, Somerset

Contents

CLIVE'S SUCCESS WAS DUE IN LARGE PART TO
THE TENACIOUS WAY HE KEPT HIS EYE ON THE BALL

We follow the same principle with our investments. So, if you're looking to help your money grow, just ring us on our free Moneyline: 0800 282 101. It could be quite an eye-opener.

**SAVE &
PROSPER**
■ THE INVESTMENT HOUSE ■
SPONSORS OF ENGLISH RUGBY

UNIT TRUSTS • PEPS • PENSIONS • SCHOOL FEES PLANS • BANKING SERVICES

Foreword

by Paul Bateman
Chief Executive
Save & Prosper Group

Firstly may I congratulate England for winning this season's Grand Slam. It gives us all at Save & Prosper great pleasure to be associated with this book celebrating England's most successful Five Nations campaign for 11 years.

Although England's victories were the result of a tremendous team effort, Rob Andrew and Dean Richards both made truly outstanding contributions. Two highlights which I shall remember in particular were Rob's complete control of the match against Scotland through his supremely accurate line-kicking, and Dean's superb performance in the second half of the game in Dublin.

It is very encouraging for us to see that since Save & Prosper started supporting rugby in 1986, of the 11 England International matches which we have sponsored, England have won nine, lost one and drawn one. There is nothing like success to breed more success and the popularity of the game at the moment is a direct result of this.

England's next major challenge is obviously the Rugby World Cup in October – a challenge for which their inspirational and dedicated captain, management and coaches have been preparing them for several years. I would like to wish them every success in that competition and would urge every England supporter to wholeheartedly support a team which is capable of beating the world's best. That competition will generate massive public interest and provide a tremendous opportunity for the game of rugby to promote itself, particularly at grass root and school levels – which of course is where our future lies.

I am confident that England will remain a major force in world rugby for some time; so much so, that Save & Prosper recently agreed to extend its sponsorship of English rugby until the end of the 1993-94 season.

Will, Rob, Dean, Geoff, Roger and the whole of the team and squad – congratulations once again. After coming so close in the last couple of seasons it is a Grand Slam well deserved.

Preparations

The defeat by Scotland at Murrayfield in March 1990 was a shattering and devastating experience for everyone in the England squad. The Triple Crown, the Calcutta Cup, the Five Nations Championship and the Grand Slam disappeared at one fell swoop. I was injured and missed the match but I knew exactly how the players felt immediately after the final whistle and throughout the inevitable post-mortems during the next few days.

The media waded into the team with a vengeance just as they had done in similar circumstances the previous March when we lost unexpectedly in the last game of the season against Wales when it had looked certain we would win that match and with it the Championship. I played in that contest and, like the rest of the side, felt completely gutted by the defeat. I appreciated the boys would have felt precisely the same at Murrayfield.

The Grand Slam of 1991 was to be seen in the context of the two last ditch failures in 1989 and 1990. Failure had given the team a ruthless determination to succeed in 1991 no matter what it took. The disastrous tour of Argentina in the summer only added to our resolve. The build-up to the Five Nations Championship should have begun in Argentina and continued in four main stages – the squad weekend at the beginning of September culminating in the match against Newcastle-Gosforth, the game against the Barbarians at the end of September, the Argentina match in November and the squad week in Lanzarote in the first week of January.

Unfortunately, the summer tour to Argentina could hardly have gone much worse. Only three of the seven matches were won which was bitterly disappointing when you consider that one of the defeats was against a club side, Banco Nacion, and two of the other losses were against the city of Buenos Aires and a district selection at Cujo, a district not apparently noted for its rugby. If that record was not bad enough the wins against Tucuman and Cordoba were each by only one score and the New Zealand All Blacks would normally expect to put 50 or 60 points on these sides without really raising a sweat.

The First Test was won convincingly but we lost the Second Test which left the deciding match in the series to be played at Twickenham in November. I was one of half-a-dozen members of the eventual Grand Slam side who did not go on the tour but that still meant that nine of our very best players took part in both Tests in Buenos Aires. The six who did not play there but who played in all four Championship games in 1991 were myself and Mike Teague in the back-row, Paul Ackford at lock and in the back division Rob Andrew, Jeremy Guscott and Rory Underwood.

What we learned from the trip to Argentina was just how weak our immediate reserve strength was. Half a dozen injuries to key players before or during the Five Nations Championship would almost certainly mean no Triple Crown or Grand Slam. Some of the players who went to Argentina will probably never be heard of again at international level, but I think a handful of the new, inexperienced guys who failed to distinguish themselves on the tour will reappear next year or the year after. As it was at the beginning of the 1990-91 season there was not a wealth of cover at full-back, fly-half, prop forward or at lock, and there was a marked difference between our first choice combination of loose forwards and the next in line.

A month after the series of setbacks in Argentina, the build-up proper started. An England President's XV strongly based on the full England squad under Geoff Cooke and Roger Uttley decamped for a long weekend to the North of England for squad training and a game against Newcastle-Gosforth. The training sessions were hard and exactly what I needed after a long lay-off, and we won the game by 32 points to 6.

It was scarcely a brilliant performance but we played well enough. Three weeks later we faced a much more daunting challenge when we took on a very powerful Barbarians side to help them celebrate their Centenary. We picked what was to be our full Grand Slam side with just two exceptions – Tony Underwood played on the wing and not Nigel Heslop and John Olver was chosen at hooker, rather than Brian Moore.

We had a long, hard session on the Saturday before the game, and in some ways the pattern for the whole season was set. We prepared for a huge forward confrontation. The Baa-Baas had All Black Ian Jones and Australian Steve Cutler at lock. That guaranteed a battle royal at the line-out. With Phil Davies at number 8 and Eric Rush at open-side flanker we knew it would be very hard to dominate the loose. And if the Barbarians won their fair share of possession they had some of the world's greatest backs to take full advantage. They had Nick Farr-Jones and Michael Lynagh, the Australian half backs, fellow Wallaby David Campese on one wing and the flying Frenchman Jean-Baptiste Lafond on the other, along with the bruising power of the All Black Joe Stanley in the centre.

We trained and planned for a very hard physical game up front and we knew then, at the end of September, that the success of the whole season was always going to depend on the crushing forward power of the England pack to relentlessly wear down the opposition and allow us to take a tactical control of events. This happened against the Barbarians and in every other match throughout the season. The style for the next five matches was established.

Paul Ackford reckons it is his ball and looks determined to keep it that way. Jason Leonard acts as minder.

Thanks mainly to the outstanding play of Paul Ackford and Wade Dooley we won more line-out ball and better quality possession. We definitely had a slight edge at the scrums in that we were more comfortable on our own ball than the Baa-Baas were on their put-in, and with this double advantage at the set-pieces we were in command in the loose.

From this set-piece domination we began to launch the driving, rolling maul at the opposition which has become our hallmark in the last couple of seasons and which has become increasingly effective. There is no doubt we do it better than any other pack in world rugby with the possible exception of the All Blacks and it certainly saps the energy of our opponents. The more our pack has played together, the better we've become at the driving maul and the more significant a part it has played in our success. We certainly posed plenty of problems for the Barbarians.

Of course we had a few advantages against the Baa-Baas. We were a fairly settled side and they were a scratch outfit full of top-class individuals but playing together as a team for the first time. We had home advantage at Twickenham. And perhaps most important of all the result meant far more to us than it did to them. To us it was a chance to get back on the rails after a series of disasters; to them it was just a great occasion for a lot of the world's best players to help a famous old club celebrate a milestone in their long and distinguished history. In the final analysis I think this was the difference between the two teams. We were desperate to win and squeezed home in an exciting match by 18 points to 16.

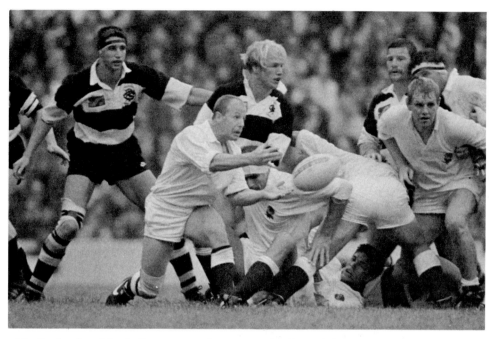

The England pack begin the season as they mean to continue, giving Richard Hill the perfect platform.

Almost by definition because of the Baa-Baas famed tradition of running rugby the game was not as tight as an international but it was keenly fought and presented us with a perfect opportunity to develop our game in preparation for the Championship in January. We introduced some new variations at the line-out, switching our main jumpers occasionally and using a few two-man line-outs, with Ackford and Dooley, and a couple of three-man line-outs where I joined the two locks. Already we had one eye on the Welsh match at Cardiff in January where we knew supremacy at the line-out was vital and well within our capability, but where two years ago we had allowed ourselves to be badly messed about.

We also adopted from set-scrums the customary New Zealand tactic of making regular use of the blind-side. Either Richard Hill or I would take off down the blind-side, the other one in support along with one of the flankers. We would run straight at the Baa-Baas wings – Campese on our right and Lafond on our left – to commit them to the tackle and the ensuing ruck or maul along with their number 8 Phil Davies and, if possible, their tearaway flanker Eric Rush. After sucking in their loose forwards, half-backs and blind-side wing, we were then ready to spin the ball wide.

The All Blacks have played to this pattern for a hundred years to great effect and it served us very well in the past season along with the superb tactical kicking of Rob Andrew and Richard Hill. The All Blacks are past masters of wearing a team down, breaking their resistance and eventually destroying them by relentlessly pounding away up front, driving non-stop in the rucks and mauls, unsparing use of the blind-side to absorb all of the five pivot players in defensive duties and good, strong, old fashioned straight running in the backs.

Some of the top international sides can survive that sort of a physical mauling for 40 minutes and even 50 or 60 minutes but precious few can stand up to such abrasive pounding for 80 minutes. The victory over the Barbarians was a terrific confidence boost to a side fighting self-doubt after Murrayfield and Argentina.

The new season had begun well with a refreshingly positive aggressive attitude. Three quarters of the pack are past the first flush of youth and it is generally accepted that in a couple of seasons perhaps only two will still be playing international rugby. 1991 had to be England's year as time was running out. The Five Nations Championship and the World Cup were the two key targets. For many it would be a last chance of glory.

The final build-up at international level before the ultimate challenge was the match against Argentina on the first Saturday in November. For this game Nigel Heslop took over from Tony Underwood and John Hall replaced Mike Teague at flank as the only two changes from the Barbarians game. The final score more or less tells the story – England 51 Argentina 0. This was one of England's biggest ever victories in an international, just a few points short of our recent record wins over Japan and Romania.

Once again and with the domestic Championship in general and the Welsh match in particular in mind, we went flat out to obliterate the Pumas pack. As pack leader I stressed the importance of producing

Nigel Heslop, one of the few successes in Argentina, continues his good form against the Pumas at Twickenham.

another grinding physical forward effort to knock the stuffing out of the Argentine pack. We outscrummaged them, cleaned them out in the line-out and we rucked and mauled them off the park. We even managed to improve on our forward display against the Barbarians.

ABOVE LEFT *Rory Underwood on his way to scoring one of his three tries against Argentina. Simon Hodgkinson is on hand, eager to supply the additional two points.*
ABOVE RIGHT *Richard Hill on the break with Dean Richards in support.*
BELOW *John Hall back in an England shirt against Argentina and leading from the front.*

Not only did our locks take a lot of superb two-handed catches at the line-out but as soon as they returned to earth we produced almost simultaneously a concerted drive to make a hole in the Pumas pack and knock them backwards on the retreat. We could then either indulge ourselves in a rolling maul or break away down the short side before releasing the backs. If the Pumas palmed the ball back, we drove through on them with fierce aggression to steamroller them towards their own line, so that when the whistle went we were automatically awarded the scrum because we were going forward.

Once we had absorbed their pivot five – the loose forwards and half-backs – in defence, covering and tackling, then we unleashed the back division who were able to extract full advantage from the glaring overlaps with which they were presented and they ran in seven spectacular tries. In fairness to the Pumas, initially they put up stiff resistance and stuck to the task throughout the match but their inexperience showed and, outgunned in terms of size, power and strength, they were eventually battered into submission.

Unfortunately, before they surrendered they delivered one knock-out blow themselves. In a very unseemly and unsavoury incident, Jeff Probyn strongly objected to being assailed by their 18-year-old schoolboy prop, Federico Mendez, and he resorted to sorting out the problem himself. Mendez then for some inexplicable reason slung a haymaker of a punch at Paul Ackford who was a completely innocent bystander looking in the opposite direction, and knocked him cold. The New Zealand referee, Colin Hawke, missed the punch but Scottish touch judge Ken McCartney did not. He attracted the referee's attention, explained what had happened and Mendez was sent off as Paul was helped off the pitch. As pack leader I had a word with Jeff Probyn, and then when Gary Rees came on as a replacement I was not best pleased at having to spend the last ten minutes of the match at lock forward in place of Paul Ackford.

In a curious sense, the punch was a back-handed compliment to England. We had outplayed the Pumas to such an extent that they had become frustrated at being submitted to such extreme forward pressure and had responded by losing their concentration, discipline and temper. That sour note apart, it was a good England performance with three tries in the last ten minutes after the departure of Mendez. In fact, we should have managed another couple of scores to break England's points-scoring record but we relaxed midway through the second half until the Mendez punch helped to concentrate our minds and lead to a renewed effort at the end.

Afterwards we agreed that despite all the good things we achieved in the match

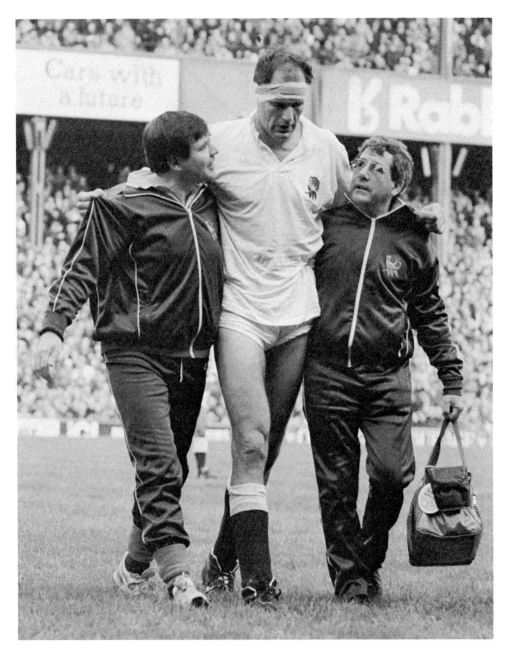

Paul Ackford, knocked out by Argentine prop Mendez, is led off by team doctor Ben Gilfeather (left) and physio Kevin Murphy. But he recovered in time to write his feature for The Observer.

if we had relaxed for twenty minutes – the way we did early in the second-half – against New Zealand or Australia, France or Scotland we would undoubtedly have paid the penalty. Geoff Cooke and Roger Uttley re-emphasised that, although it was a good win, if we were really serious about winning Championships and Triple Crowns and Grand Slams we would have to exert control and total concentration not just for 50 or 60 minutes but for the whole 80 minutes. On the credit side, after the slating in the press in Buenos Aires in August, it was very reassuring to enjoy such an emphatic, comprehensive win.

The previous week Ireland had only managed to beat Argentina in Dublin with a penalty goal in injury time which suggested that we were a long way ahead of the Irish. The week after our success at Twickenham Scotland achieved a victory over the Pumas on a par with ours and France put up a reasonable show against New Zealand in Paris which confirmed our early season thoughts that the two hardest matches in the Five Nations Championship would be against Scotland and France even though both these games would be our two home matches at Twickenham.

The rest of November was taken up with a couple of Courage League games and the first three Saturdays of December were devoted to the Divisional Championship. During that period I was in regular contact with Geoff Cooke, Roger Uttley and Will Carling to discuss the preparations for the opening Championship game in Cardiff, but the final touches were put together in the first week of January when the whole squad went to Lanzarote.

We trained hard for two sessions each day in the morning and afternoon and spent each evening watching videos of previous important games before launching into a tactical discussion aimed primarily at the Welsh match. I was directly involved in the team planning as leader of the forwards along with the captain, Will Carling, and the manager and coach but, in fact, they were mostly very open discussions and everyone chipped in.

Lanzarote provided a mixture of physical and tactical preparation for the four internationals and it was deemed a great success because the training conditions were ideal. There were none of the distractions which we would inevitably have suffered if we had spent a week at a training camp in England and the weather was, of course, much better in the Canary Islands. The management planning was extremely thorough even to the extent that every player was given an audio tape which had been recorded by a sports psychologist explaining what our approach should be to facing Wales in Cardiff, where we had failed to win since 1963.

It was a perfectly sensible idea but I have to confess that despite Geoff Cooke pointing out we would all be questioned on the tape at the end of the week I never got round to listening to it because firstly I needed absolutely no special motivation to want to beat Wales in Cardiff, Twickenham or anywhere else for that matter and secondly I was very confident we were a much better side than this particular Welsh team. Wales announced their side whilst we were in Lanzarote and it was near enough what we had expected.

We had watched videos of our wins over the Barbarians and Argentina to see the specific areas where we needed to improve and to analyse our own strengths and weaknesses. We also watched and examined videos of previous recent matches against Wales to look at their strengths and weaknesses. This was all part of our ruthless determination to lay once and for all the bogey of Cardiff which had haunted many of our players in the 1980s.

We had certain major advantages which had to be exploited. It was generally accepted that we had a better, stronger set of forwards in almost every single area and both before and after the match in Cardiff, on radio, television and in the papers, the media pointed out that if a composite pack was chosen from the combined talents of the 16 English and Welsh forwards not a single Welsh player would have been chosen. This situation gave us a great deal of confidence which was further increased in a key area of international rugby where we had a huge bonus – experience.

The Welsh had precious little experience in their pack with a whole lot of relative newcomers and not a single British Lion amongst them. We had a wealth of experience including six British Lions, and no matter how good or promising a new player is experience counts for a great deal at international level.

We had been guilty of being a trifle naive when we lost at Cardiff in 1989 because the Welsh succeeded in reducing the line-out to a shambolic lottery. This time we were determined to be in command and continued to develop a whole range of variations to ensure control in this crucial area. We knew Paul Ackford and Wade Dooley would clean up in a straightforward jumping contest and so we worked hard at our two and three man line-outs as well as tightening up at full seven-man lines. If the ball had to be palmed rather than caught two-handed on occasions, then players were delegated and organised to tidy up at once and the rest of the pack immediately had to re-group and begin the juggernaut drive forward. Ackford and Dooley as a partnership are the best locks in the world and we had to make certain that in Cardiff they were allowed to exploit to the full their huge advantage.

In the set scrums, England can rightly boast the best front row in Europe and Jason Leonard, Brian Moore and Jeff Probyn are also as good a combination as any in the Southern Hemisphere. The way Jason has come through his baptism by fire at a relatively young age for a prop has been a huge plus for England. The phenomenal scrummaging of Jeff Probyn has also been very important.

As we trained in Lanzarote we knew that our loose forward blend was very good and each player complemented the particular skills of the other two. After so many matches and squad sessions together Peter Winterbottom, Mike Teague and myself knew each other's play inside out whereas all the other countries in the Championship were playing new back-row combinations.

On the assumption that our pack would generally be rolling forward and making life relatively easy for our backs we were still fortunate that we were able to field such a strong back division. After a few hiccups in recent years, we were able to field the best half-backs in the Northern Hemisphere both individually and, most importantly, as a partnership.

Rob Andrew, ever since the British Lions tour of 1989, has developed into an outstanding fly-half who can do everything. He is a tremendous tackler, superb kicker of the ball, confidently chooses the right options in attack, has excellent hands and can either play to the pack or set the threequarters free. Richard Hill has the fastest, most accurate service of the current crop of international scrum-halves and is one of the few Northern Hemisphere players who would walk straight into the current New Zealand side. He is also very good in defence, he covers and tackles like an extra flanker and his tactical kicking is top-notch.

If our pack was going to have an off day in the Championship, it was extremely reassuring to know that we had so many match-winners behind the scrum. Will Carling and Jeremy Guscott must rate as just about the best attacking centre pairing in world rugby and in defence they give nothing away. Rory Underwood has been one of the best three wings in the world for the past four years along with David Campese of Australia and John Kirwan of New Zealand. He is now at the peak of his career and even from limited opportunities is absolutely lethal in attack as befits the top try-scorer for England. Nigel Heslop is a strong, resolute runner and aggressive defender and Simon Hodgkinson has a fantastic record as a goal-kicker.

As we wound up our training in Lanzarote and completed our build-up for the Championship, there was every reason for confidence and optimism. We believed that our backs were definitely the best in the four Home Unions and on a par with the French. We also believed that our forwards were at least 20 per cent better than any of the other four sides in the Championship. It was up to us to go out and prove this during the ensuing two months beginning against Wales in Cardiff.

Victory
in Cardiff

Cardiff Arms Park
Saturday 19th January

WALES 6 ENGLAND 25

Wales England

Wales		England
P.H. THORBURN (captain) Neath	15	**S.D. HODGKINSON** Nottingham
I.C. EVANS Llanelli	14	**N.J. HESLOP** Orrell
M.G. RING Cardiff	13	**W.D.C. CARLING (captain)** Harlequins
I.S. GIBBS Neath	12	**J.C. GUSCOTT** Bath
S.P. FORD Cardiff	11	**R. UNDERWOOD** Leicester
N.R. JENKINS Pontypridd	10	**C.R. ANDREW** Wasps
R.N. JONES Swansea	9	**R.J. HILL** Bath
B.R. WILLIAMS Neath	1	**J. LEONARD** Harlequins
K.H. PHILLIPS Neath	2	**B.C. MOORE** Harlequins
P. KNIGHT Pontypridd	3	**J.A. PROBYN** Wasps
G.D. LLEWELLYN Neath	4	**P.J. ACKFORD** Harlequins
G.O. LLEWELLYN Neath	5	**W.A. DOOLEY** Preston Grasshoppers
A.J. CARTER Newport	6	**M.C. TEAGUE** Gloucester
P. ARNOLD Swansea	7	**P.J. WINTERBOTTOM** Harlequins
G.M. GEORGE Newport	8	**D. RICHARDS** Leicester

REPLACEMENTS		REPLACEMENTS
C.J. BRIDGES (Neath)	16	**J.M. WEBB** (Bath)
D.W. EVANS (Cardiff)	17	**D.P. HOPLEY** (Wasps)
A. CLEMENT (Swansea)	18	**C.D. MORRIS** (Orrell)
K. WATERS (Newbridge)	19	**P.A.G. RENDALL** (Wasps)
E. LEWIS (Llanelli)	20	**C.J. OLVER** (Northampton)
M. GRIFFITHS (Cardiff)	21	**M.G. SKINNER** (Harlequins)

REFEREE: **R. Megson (Scotland)**

Wales 6   England 25

SCORERS

Penalties: Thorburn, Jenkins

SCORERS

Try Teague

Penalties Hodgkinson (7)

That England recorded their biggest ever victory in Wales was an achievement which failed to gain the recognition it deserved. There were two reasons for this. Firstly, the game itself was of such a poor standard that there were few great moments for the impartial observer to savour. Secondly, most of the post-match media attention focussed on the boycotting of the press conference by the England captain and management. The ostensible reason given was that there had been too much hype surrounding the previous season's Championship campaign; this created an undue level of interest which the management felt had worked against the team in the Grand Slam game at Murrayfield. Quite simply, the fact that England were made overwhelming favourites had motivated Scotland to success. There was a desire to keep a lower profile this time around. This was an understandable aim, but utterly naive in its execution. The media got a much better story than they would ever have had. Mixed in with all this was a dispute between the squad and the BBC, the latter claiming that a sum of £5,000 had been requested for post-match interviews. The BBC refused, the players kept silent and the RFU were outraged. So much for the low-key strategy.

At least the on-field strategy met with more success. There were flaws, there were errors and there were areas of weakness. But Wales never looked like winning the game. They were beaten in Cardiff for the first time in 28 years and full-back Simon Hodgkinson kicked a world record seven penalties. The latter statistic gave a true indication of the match itself. England dominated both territory and possession, thereby exerting terrific pressure on their opponents whose only answer was to infringe. Mike Teague's try fifteen minutes from time came from a scrum near the Welsh line and was a fitting reward for a fine performance from the Gloucester flanker who had only regained his place at the expense of the injured John Hall.

Local strength. Fully international.

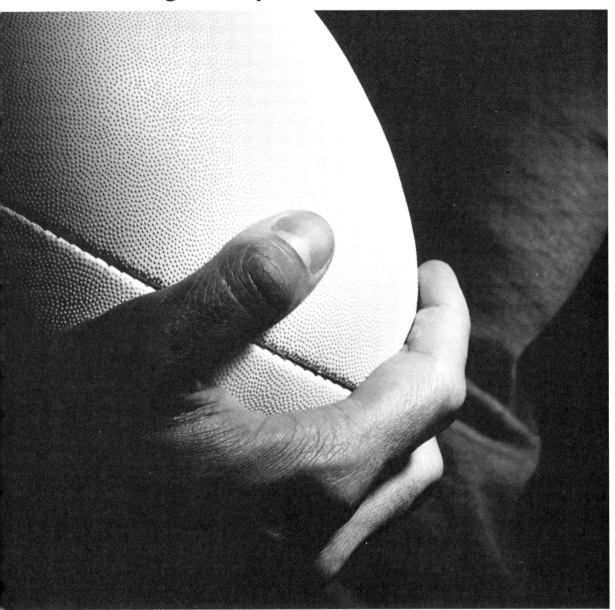

The top players have a number of things in common.

Experience of playing conditions around the world. A capacity to read the game. A sense of team-work. Strength. Speed. And, above all, the ability to make fast decisions.

The Five Nations Championship strides suddenly into your head. In December it is no more than a distant thought. By January it is a huge shadow beginning to fall over you. By mid-Championship it is difficult to find a sleeping moment, let alone a waking one, when it is not on your mind. I wouldn't have it any other way. It's the best time of the year.

I had been busy in December. I was captain of London in the Divisionals, then there was Xmas itself with a five-month-old daughter to consider for the first time in life, followed by the Barbarians game at Leicester. I prefer to be busy. Too much idle time leaves too much time for negative thinking. During the build-up to a game I often spend Friday afternoon after training making 'phone calls to the office, not just to keep the boss sweet, but because I find that allowing the game to weigh too heavily is counter-productive. Long live amateurism, in whatever form it may take, because I would not want to have rugby dominate my entire life. Most of it, yes; but not all of it.

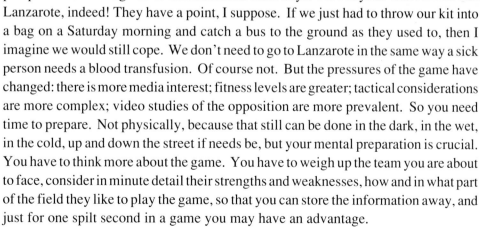

And so to January. And so to Lanzarote. I can hear some of the old players turning and grumbling in their grave, bemoaning the pampered treatment given to internationals these days. Five days in Lanzarote, indeed! They have a point, I suppose. If we just had to throw our kit into a bag on a Saturday morning and catch a bus to the ground as they used to, then I imagine we would still cope. We don't need to go to Lanzarote in the same way a sick person needs a blood transfusion. Of course not. But the pressures of the game have changed: there is more media interest; fitness levels are greater; tactical considerations are more complex; video studies of the opposition are more prevalent. So you need time to prepare. Not physically, because that still can be done in the dark, in the wet, in the cold, up and down the street if needs be, but your mental preparation is crucial. You have to think more about the game. You have to weigh up the team you are about to face, consider in minute detail their strengths and weaknesses, how and in what part of the field they like to play the game, so that you can store the information away, and just for one spilt second in a game you may have an advantage.

Lanzarote this year was very successful. Facilities are good there, the weather is usually warm and sunny and the England boys are a good bunch to be with. I am sure most players would say that about team-mates but in my experience this is the most harmonious group I have played with at international level. It's like a club side. We have been together a long while now: we know each other; we respect each other and we are friends with each other. It means a lot.

The Grand Slam defeat in 1990 set the tone for the whole season. I could sense it in Lanzarote. It was not articulated as such, but you could feel that strong sense of grievance. Not that we had been robbed on the day because we hadn't been. Scotland had beaten us fair and square. But there was a definite feeling that we owed ourselves and our supporters something better. We were not being arrogant but we felt we merited a Grand Slam. No-one said it: they didn't need to. The eyes said it all. This was going to be a hard season but we were not going to be beaten. We were not going to blow it again.

The first game is always difficult. Five Nations rugby is a different pace entirely. It is far, far faster than league games and a significant step up even from divisional standard. There is another factor. Preparing for an international is different. We never spend time away from home for a club game, apart from the occasional cup match. Yet here we are, every fortnight in the Championship, spending Saturday night and Sunday morning together before being closeted from Wednesday onwards. It's unreal and takes some getting used to. At least soccer players are in the habit of overnight stays in their league games whilst cricketers spend more time in hotels than they do on the field in some wet summers. For rugby players, it is a different experience.

This squad has at least got used to it all. How to fill the time; how to get on with your room-mate and not suffocate him if he snores – Richard Hill doesn't – and how to pace your build-up correctly and not burn yourself out. We had our usual squad session the weekend before the Welsh game. At the start of the campaign it is vital to get as much time on the field as possible: by the end of the season, Sunday training might be considered superfluous. On a couple of occasions this season Geoff Cooke proposed that we scrap it simply because of all the travelling involved. He had no chance. We are creatures of habit. Even if sometimes it might not be of massive importance, we felt we ought to do it, just in case. Paranoia is never far below the surface of any sportsman.

We had all had league matches the day before, so the amount of hard contact work that Sunday at Twickenham before the Welsh game was minimal. We ran through drills; covered set pieces. Richard and I did a few lengths together. All good simple stuff. The mind begins to focus; the body steels itself and the butterflies start to stretch a little wing or two.

There was little doubt that we all felt good physically. We had been this way before and knew that we had the fitness, the strength and the skills to compete and to win. Had we got it right in the head? Wales would be a big psychological hurdle. I never discussed the possibility of losing with Richard Hill, but we both sensed that little nagging voice somewhere in the room. What if we lost to Wales? Where would we go from there? Would there be any point going anywhere? The season would be over. That was the stark truth of the matter. The other games we could make excuses for if we lost: Scotland were Grand Slam champions: Ireland in Dublin are a force possessed and France are France. But Wales; no disrespect, but we had beaten them 34-6 the year before and they were in a terrible state. Our credibility would be blown sky high if we lost.

But we wouldn't lose, would we? That little voice would not go away. Just as it had haunted every English team for the past 28 years, so it echoed around us. Not very loudly, but it was there. That is why it was absolutely right to confront the 'Cardiff jinx' right from the beginning. We knew as early as Lanzarote that we were going to make a break from tradition and stay in Cardiff from Thursday evening onwards. However we were not prepared for what hit us at Wednesday training in Gloucester. As we trotted out on to the pitch, the tannoy crackled into life. *Hen wlad vy nhadai...*, the Welsh anthem boomed out, much to the amusement of the group of supporters, red-dragon flags wrapped around them, who taunted us from one corner of the ground. I must admit that a few of us thought it was no more than a bit of fun. But it did the trick. Whatever little cracks we made that evening about 'Cookie' having finally flipped, he got it right. We needed to confront the whole myth of Welsh invincibility right from the outset. The battle song which had supposedly struck so much terror into the hearts of Englishmen down the years was no more than a cheap cassette crackling out from the Kingsholm tannoy.

We have always said to the media that the Cardiff bogey was no problem for us. Deep down we knew it was a factor. Geoff recognised that. He changed all our normal plans in order to confront the problem. We drove into Cardiff on Thursday evening. Normally we stay out at the cloistered grounds of St Pierre in Chepstow. They are lovely surroundings, quiet, secluded, cut off from intruders and totally unreal. This is not the ideal preparation. You need to see the way the Welsh feel about the English. Otherwise when you drive in on a Saturday morning, it hits you hard. Too hard for some in years past, who never quite came to terms with the force of those feelings. Cardiff Arms Park is not like other grounds. It's right there in the middle of the city. The place is teeming on a Saturday and it's an intimidating sight.

This year we were in there face-to-face with the opposition, seen, unseen; real and imagined. If the ghosts of a thousand humbled English players were floating around Cardiff, we wanted to meet them and look them in the eye. So too the real enemy. We met Welshmen in the hotel foyer, in the lift and in the street. There was banter in the exchanges for the most part, but there is always an undercurrent. We were acclimatising.

We trained at Wycliffe College in Gloucester that Thursday morning. It was behind closed doors. Geoff had decided to follow the pattern of the other countries and have one of the sessions off limits. No cameras, no press, no radio microphones and I must say it was a nice change. Of course, it is no more than a slight irritant to have to talk to the press, and on many occasions it is a pleasure, but it depends just when it occurs. If 50 media folk turn up, you are honour bound to talk to them all. It was nice just to get there, train and leave.

199 to go.

Richard Hill and I like to finish a session on our own. Whilst Simon Hodgkinson does his goal-kicking stuff at one end of the field, Richard will line up a dozen balls and away we go. I'll catch and kick: or catch and pass; or occasionally catch and drop. We will do 200 passes. It is something that Richard instigated and he does it every day. He likes to practise and, although I never used to bother about practising that much, now I too draw great comfort as well as benefit from the routine. We always take a separate car to these sessions so that we don't keep the other guys hanging around. Richard drove us back to the Crest Hotel in Gloucester. We showered, had lunch and headed for Wales.

The Crest Hotel overlooks the ground. This was my fourth match against Wales in Cardiff. I had heard all the hype before: no win in 22 years, no win in 24 years, no win in 26 years. Now it was 28 years. Would it ever end? At that point I felt it would. The little voice of doubt was having an evening off. Training had gone well and I liked the idea of being in where the action was. On Thursday evenings after dinner we always have a video session. Now, if ever there were a phrase which gives a false impression of what really goes on, it is that one: 'a video session'. No, not 'Top Gun', or 'Mary Poppins', feet up, start snoring half way through. Our video work is very intensive. Geoff Cooke, Roger Uttley and Don Rutherford will have edited several tapes, stringing together various points about the opposition. This time round it was a question of familiarisation. Who was Neil Jenkins? Who was Scott Gibbs? Who were Carter and George, the two flankers? That may sound somewhat patronising but it is not meant to be. I, and most of the players, had never seen these guys play, let alone play against them. I wanted to know which foot Jenkins favoured; which side he liked to run towards; what angle and at what speed the back-row came off. It all sounds rather straightforward but there are so many different patterns to a game. You need to know them all.

We were aiming to try and put pressure on Jenkins in this his first game. Not so much by me running at him or anything. Fly-halves don't tend to go head-to-head. The best way would be to disrupt the supply of ball so that Jenkins would receive it under pressure. Our forwards were capable of doing that and that is what we discussed. Bed Thursday night and it felt good.

That optimistic mood carried over into Friday morning. Training was at Sophia Gardens and there was a huge crowd there – supporters as well as media. We wanted to impress, not that it would make any real difference to things on the day, but we felt like putting on a show. It was all part of this new approach. Friday sessions in Wales were usually very tame affairs. You were not going to do much anyway and out at Chepstow there would just be a few press guys milling around. All very low-key. Here in Cardiff there was an atmosphere and we thrived on it. We stayed out for about an hour.

Then came the worst part. The 24-hour wait for kick-off. Time drags. No doubt about it. If you let it get to you, it can destroy you. That is why I like to make a few phone calls to work. It keeps my mind occupied. Of course I am thinking about the game, but not too much. That Friday afternoon I went across the road to the Arms Park, through the Cardiff club ground and into the National Stadium. Brian Moore and John Olver were over the other side of the pitch. They made the mistake of walking across for a chat. The groundsman went bananas. Sensitive breed, groundsmen. Let 30 guys rip the guts out of a pitch for 80 minutes on a Saturday and they don't mind, but two guys in flat shoes on a Friday afternoon is a different story.

It had begun raining heavily so I nipped round to the Cardiff office of Debenham, Tewson and Chinnocks, the firm of chartered surveyors I work for in London. I was out off the rain at least. The weather is always a factor in these games. It can make a big difference. On a wet day the ball will come to you that little bit more slowly: you will take a split second longer to grip it just to make sure it doesn't slip, so that, down the line, you have a much slower pace to the passing. We looked at the forecast on Friday evening. It should blow over. If not, we faced the same prospect as two years earlier when, in wet conditions, Robert Jones had kicked us to defeat.

By Friday evening the tension had begun to mount but we were in good spirits. Team talks are very player orientated. This has been one of Geoff Cooke's great strengths – getting the players to think things through for themselves. Will Carling picks on different guys to address the group, getting them to put their perspective on the game ahead. Richard Hill, Mike Teague and Rory Underwood had their say this time. Three different men: one simple message. We had to be mentally prepared. If we were in the right frame of mind then we only had to do the simple things and our greater experience and class would tell. Dinner, a game of pool for some, television for others, and so to bed. We were ready.

By Saturday morning, something had changed. The balance had shifted. Before we were tense, but not too tense. That even keel was gone. Even at breakfast it was obvious we were uptight. The voice of doubt was back. And what a noise it was making. The fear of losing was upon us. Even I felt nervous. I thought that after so many years I was getting used to the international scene but my stomach was churning. Significantly it continued to do so long after the final whistle and into the night. That had never happened before. Now, if I was that fraught, some of the others must have been close to exploding. It was obvious what had happened. The ghosts of Murrayfield 1990 had come to haunt us that morning. If we lost here, that was that. We had never won anything, and if we lost today we never would.

Still, we put on a brave face. We were in a pretty grim mood. There was none of the usual banter at the team talks. In hindsight it was this desperate determination not to lose that drove us to the Grand Slam. This was its first manifestation. It might have cramped our rugby on occasions but it definitely got us through the bad times, particularly in Dublin. No-one was going to beat us.

The final meeting was at about 1 o'clock and there was not a sound in the room, save the pounding beat of twenty-one hearts. We walked to the ground. It was a part of the great scheme not to be intimidated by things. In truth it was simple sense. The ground was no more than a few hundred yards away. Symbolically, it did us good, particularly the forwards. Their game is all about confrontation. Here they were, not being affected one bit by the atmosphere. Or so it appeared. Inside they were churning.

The build-up had been close to perfect. No-one even flinched at the anthems. What was all the fuss about? Within a minute of the start we found out. We won the

ABOVE *The England front row, already in the ascendancy, can't wait to scrum down against Wales.*
BELOW RIGHT *The Llewellyn brothers, sandwiched between Ackford and Dooley, came off second best most of the afternoon.*
BELOW LEFT *Neil Jenkins, who had a good first match in difficult circumstances, was always trying to give his backs a chance.*

toss and chose to kick off. I did a funny one to the right, away from the forwards. It landed near the new cap, Scott Gibbs. Perfect. Our forwards piled in to give him a hammering and it looked good. That was until they piled right over him and conceded a penalty. First touch for Neil Jenkins. He fluffed it, the ball was sliced and underneath was Dean Richards, the safest hands in the world. He dropped it, Wales poured forward, Robert Jones box-kicked, now we were under pressure, conceded a penalty, Thorburn kicked it, we were 3-0 down and the whole of Wales was going potty. I remember running back under the posts to face the kick thinking, 'This can't be happening'.

It was. The spectre of yet another unexpected defeat began to loom. Five years ago that sort of start would have knocked the stuffing out of us. This time we were prepared to fight back. Like all sides, we needed luck. We made maximum use of

Will Carling, confronted by Ring, finds plenty of support from Teague and Leonard.

our opportunities, Simon Hodgkinson slotting them over with ease whilst at the other end Paul Thorburn was having a wretched afternoon. I don't honestly think that even if Paul had kicked those goals, to bring the scores closer, that we would ever have lost.

We were not playing well, it's true. I was not kicking well and the ball was often landing short, whilst Richard, for his part, was tending to over-hit straight to Thorburn. But up front you sensed that the game was ours. And if we got ahead, there was no way we were going to let go. We got to 18-6 and from then on I was happy to keep the gate shut. We had come to Cardiff to win. It was as simple as that.

Back in the dressing-room you would have thought we had lost. No-one said a word. That horrible knot in the stomach was still there. For whatever reason, we had obviously become a bit too wound up. The anxiety had affected our play and we were not happy with our performance.

If you could have seen the dismal scene, you might have been able to appreciate why none of us fancied facing the media. That doesn't justify our action; it just explains it. The whole aftermath was a rather sorry affair; not because I think the boycott was wrong, but because there was so much misunderstanding about it all. In part that was our fault. There were four factors:

1 the rather unreal atmosphere before and after the game.
2 a genuine desire to keep a lower profile this year. We had not done any interviews on the Friday because we had seen what had happened at Murrayfield the previous year when the press took all our comments out of context and made us out to be a real arrogant bunch.
3 frustration with a few over-intrusive sections of the media
4 the supposed £5,000 fee we had demanded from the BBC. In fact most of us genuinely knew nothing about this. That was a separate negotiation conducted by our agents, the Willis brothers, with whom we subsequently parted company.

Traditionally relationships with the press have been good. They still are. In fact the following Monday we had a clear-the-air meeting with some of them at The Stoop Memorial Ground, just to put over our point of view and to assure them that there had been a misunderstanding. Nevertheless our desire for a lower profile was genuine. Perhaps we were naive in the way we went about it: but it was well-meant. (Most players have a rather contradictory stance towards the media, claiming that they don't take much notice of what is written and then ordering every newspaper available when they arrive at the team hotel on a Wednesday evening.)

Robert Jones makes good use of some rare Welsh possession.

We are wary of saying anything that might be misrepresented, knowing that a banner headline in one of the tabloids is often a distortion purely to grab attention. And yet we very quickly latch on to any opponent's comments in the press, using them to motivate ourselves, despite knowing full well that he probably had not said it like that in the first place. You pays your money... As it was I think that in the long term the boycott may have done us some good. It showed that there were a few issues to thrash out and it did no harm to make that point. As for it taking the shine of our victory – that's nonsense. Nothing could do that. A victory in Cardiff does not happen that often.

I ought to have been looking forward to the Five Nations Championship but I wasn't. I had missed all the previous season with a shoulder injury and, even though I had actually enjoyed the rest, I still welcomed having a chance to be back in the frame again. No matter how laid-back I may appear, I relish the challenge of playing at the top level. The harder, the better; the more difficult, the better. It's what any sportsman wants: to pit himself against the best and come out a winner. The rest of it I can do without: the hype, the publicity, the attention, even the training. But give me the 80 minutes, 15 against 15, preferably in the middle of nowhere, and I love it.

Why wasn't I loving it at this point then, just a few days before the opener against Wales? Simple: I was injured. Not only had I struggled through most of the last month with an ankle injury, picked up when playing for the Midlands against the North, but I had also strained my calf muscle in Lanzarote. It was touch and go whether I would make it at all. I got a game in for Leicester the week before, and that was basically all I did in over a month. Now, as I am not the world's greatest trainer anyway, that left me a little bit short of fitness. I rely on playing for my fitness, be it rugby, 5-a-side football, squash, badminton or chasing crooks through Hinckley on a Saturday night. I kept the extent of the calf injury quiet. Geoff Cooke knew I was struggling but he also knew he could trust my judgement. I reckoned I could just about make it. I was however praying for a filthy wet day, six inches of mud, with the ball not going much further than my outside boot at a scrummage.

I enjoyed being back in the England set-up simply because they were a good bunch of boys to play rugby with. There is no pretension about them: they just get on, do their stuff and don't moan about things. The two days before the match were spent in familiarisation: getting used to the line-out calls, the scrummage positions and the back-row moves. Most of it we have done a hundred times before in years past, but it still needs those few hours together to make it sharp again. There is very little room for error at this level and if your binding is a little bit adrift in the scrummage it can cost you dearly. I think that showed against Wales. With all due respect they were not a good pack and as Scotland had showed they had weaknesses in the tight. We never really exploited that, so obviously we had work to do in that area for our next match.

It is the same with the line-out. Quite apart from whether Ackford or Dooley gets off the ground, there are a whole host of other facets that need regular attention. The blocking, the driving, the tidying up and, crucially, the awareness to get the second touch. You have to practise picking up deflections, making sure that you can anticipate the nudge and be in the right position. This was where I fell down badly in Cardiff. This was where my lack of match sharpness really showed. Usually I am quite good at snatching the deflections. Against Wales nothing stuck at all. I was just not on my toes.

Despite my own problems I felt fairly confident about the team's chances against Wales. Of course you have to be confident about facing any opponent. Why bother going in there at all if there's no real belief in the belly? However that sense of optimism is tempered by varying degrees of respect for the opposition. It was hard to feel too much for Wales. They had been very poor against England the year before and there was nothing in their build-up to suggest that we would be unduly troubled. It's true we had lost 12-9 there two years ago but their side had deteriorated since then. No Bob Norster for a start and that was a very big difference. It may sound arrogant to dismiss them so lightly but you have to be realistic. If I felt there was one hell of a battle in prospect, then I would have been quite happy to admit so. As it was I could not see any way we would lose.

Not even because of the 28-year voodoo. It preyed on the minds of others more than it did with me. I try to be a bit more down-to-earth about these things. It doesn't matter what happens off the field, be it in your favour or against you, once the whistle blows there is a game to be won or lost. It is as simple as that. Psychological preparation has never interested me unduly. The tapes that Geoff Cooke handed out about visualisation, goal-setting and the like went straight in the bin I am afraid. That sort of thing might work for some: it doesn't for me. The Welsh anthem at Kingsholm on Wednesday night was no more than a bit of fun. That is the way I took it anyway. By the time it was played for real on Saturday afternoon, we were singing along to it. I can accept that that was probably Geoff's intention and acknowledge that for some of the younger boys it might have been important.

Wales is always a bit of a tricky place to visit. There is not a lot of love lost between the two countries: a relationship based on trust and understanding, as the old

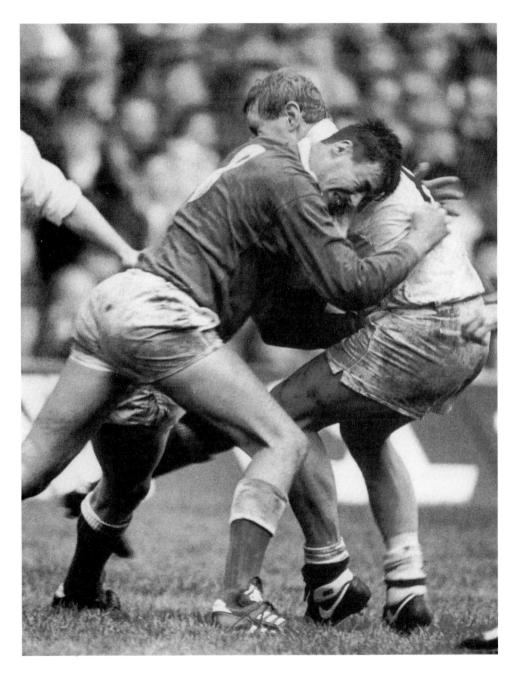

Dean Richards protects the ball as Paul Arnold weighs in.

line goes. They don't trust us and we don't understand them. Taking us into the heart of Cardiff on the Thursday was a different tack about which I had mixed feelings. I quite like the peace and quiet of Chepstow. Certainly it beats being woken up at 3 a.m. two nights running by Welshmen singing lullabies outside your bedroom window. Of all the away venues Dublin is my favourite. People are genuinely friendly. They hope that their side knocks the living daylights out of you but that you have a good time as well. They've got the attitude just right. Paris I also like because it has its own special atmosphere; loud, hostile and intimidating. Murrayfield has become a bit like Cardiff Arms Park in a way. There is a very anti-English feeling in the air these days. But it's only a game when all is said and done, and if people get off on really baying for your blood then that is their problem.

Killing time was no real worry in Wales. The hotel had a full-sized snooker table and so competition began. To the fore were the policemen, a sure sign of misspent work time. Ackford and Dooley have the benefit of being based at large police stations in Clapham and Blackpool, both of which have tables, whereas us poor country cousins at Hinckley have to do some real work and have no time or space for such luxuries. That is my excuse for playing so poorly anyway.

The hours before the game, as all the players will admit, are the worst. I head for the card table, usually with Jerry Guscott, for a game of cribbage. It's either that, a video or a kip. If you have come into England training after working a series of night shifts, it takes time catch up on your sleep. Apart from that, I am a lazy beggar anyway and would probably drop of for a snooze even during a video. That Friday afternoon it was 'Henry V', all good stirring stuff.

By Saturday morning I could sense that some of the boys were a bit tense but that was to be expected. First game and all that. The forwards meeting at 11 o'clock just went through all

Chaos reigns as the forwards fall over each other in pursuit of the ball.

TOP *Richard Hill leaves the Welsh and referee Ray Megson in his wake.*
ABOVE *Kevin Phillips, on the brink of defeat, tries to rally his exhausted pack.*
RIGHT *Mike Teague spurred on by Paul Ackford enjoys his moment of glory - scoring the only try of the match.*

the calls. I don't envy Richard Hill his having to remember the signals for both backs and forwards. Brian Moore will call the shots in the line-out whilst I will liaise with Richard and Rob on whether the ball will run or be worked through the back-row. I get involved in that simply because I am number 8. As pack leader I am fairly redundant, even at training sessions. The side are too experienced to need me to direct operations. 'Ackers' knows when he wants the ball: so does Wade. As for geeing people up through the game, I am just too tired to do that. They are all big boys: they drive themselves.

First-class rugby is hard. That is part of the appeal, the physical confrontation. Obviously there is a line between legitimate and illegitimate aggression. Sometimes you step over that line. Players know when that transgression is just a bit of temper, over in a flash and unimportant. They also know when it's premeditated and done to put you off your game or, far worse, out of the game. There is no point pretending it doesn't go on because it does and you have to be ready for it. I do think, however, that there is probably more skulduggery at junior level than senior. Certainly at international level there are so many eyes watching – the ref, the touch judges, the TV, the crowd – that it is almost impossible to get away with it. Mind you, the French don't seem to do too badly. In our meeting that morning it was the usual message: we had more to lose by getting rattled. There had been ill-tempered games in Cardiff – 1987, after which four players were suspended, and 1989, when Mike Teague lasted five seconds. So we had to be on our guard. Let the referee sort it out: then if he didn't, it was the usual, one in, all in. That may sound a cliché, but intimidation does go on and you have to be ready to stand your ground. We also made a point of trying to be nice to the referee. We would not query decisions, would be polite when asking for clarification and generally not be a pain in his side. I have no idea whether it ever makes any difference, but you never know.

What a start. I had no excuse for dropping that high ball early on which allowed them to set up position for the penalty. That was the beginning of a miserable afternoon for me. I could have had no complaints if I had been dropped after that performance. I played like a drain: off the pace in the loose and unable to get the first touch on all the loose balls. It was the worst game I had played for England: one to forget, that's for sure. Luckily the side around me were so good that they were able to cover my deficiencies. Even though we were 3-0 down so early I had no worries. After about ten minutes I realised the game was ours for the taking. You can tell by

Carling and Guscott wonder why it had been so difficult for the past 28 years.

the contact in the tackle and in the loose whether you have got the whip hand. Wales didn't really believe in themselves. We soon sorted out the barging in the line-outs by cutting down to two men, and although we were not on top of our form we had enough in reserve to be comfortable. It was a strange match in a way. Wales were so poor that at the final whistle I didn't know whether to be ecstatic, relieved, smug, or sympathetic. It was a record win for England yet some of their players didn't seem to be too bothered by it. I couldn't understand that. If England lost by that margin I would have wanted to hide away for a week. Yet some, not all, but some players that night at the dinner were still quite full of themselves. Small wonder that they are in trouble.

I am not a big one for immediate post-match analysis. I am too shattered to think straight and the serious appraisal can wait until the next time we meet up. I am all for a few beers and a quiet chat. You need time to unwind. As for the post-match press boycott, I knew little about what was going on. I prefer to keep a low profile. I don't like any of the hype, even when we have won well and the papers are full of praise. That said, I do recognise that there is a responsibility to deal with the media. The public want to know what a certain player feels about the game and they have a right to know. It helps promote the game as well and that is important. What is not on though is being woken up at 11 o'clock at night or 7:30 in the morning by the *Outer Hebrides Biennial Gazette* asking for an in-depth interview. There is a time and a place, and if we can get that established things will be much better. It did not worry me one bit that the press made so much of it all on Monday except that some were claiming that we wanted £5,000. No-one knew about that. It was a separate deal which I only learned about when a reporter rang me on Sunday afternoon.

I was glad to get that Wales of the way. It was not a great or a pretty game. We had gone to do a job and we had done it, so I wasn't too worried about the style. We could have played better so there was plenty to work on. But that could wait. First, there was a little bit of skiing for me to enjoy.

The Calcutta Cup

Twickenham
Saturday 16th February

ENGLAND 21 SCOTLAND 12

England Scotland

England		Scotland
S.D. HODGKINSON Nottingham	15	**A.G. HASTINGS** Watsonians
N.J. HESLOP Orrell	14	**A.G. STANGER** Hawick
W.D.C. CARLING (captain) Harlequins	13	**S. HASTINGS** Watsonians
J.C. GUSCOTT Bath	12	**S.R.P. LINEEN** Boroughmuir
R. UNDERWOOD Leicester	11	**A. MOORE** Edinburgh Academicals
C.R. ANDREW Wasps	10	**C.M. CHALMERS** Melrose
R.J. HILL Bath	9	**G. ARMSTRONG** Jed-Forest
J. LEONARD Harlequins	1	**D.M.B. SOLE (captain)** Edinburgh Academicals
B.C. MOORE Harlequins	2	**K.S. MILNE** Heriot's F.P.
J.A. PROBYN Wasps	3	**A.P. BURNELL** London Scottish
P.J. ACKFORD Harlequins	4	**C.A. GRAY** Nottingham
W.A. DOOLEY Preston Grasshoppers	5	**D.F. CRONIN** Bath
M.C. TEAGUE Gloucester	6	**D.J. TURNBULL** Hawick
P.J. WINTERBOTTOM Harlequins	7	**J. JEFFREY** Kelso
D. RICHARDS Leicester	8	**D.B. WHITE** London Scottish

REPLACEMENTS		REPLACEMENTS
J.M. WEBB (Bath)	16	**P.W. DODS** (Gala)
S.J. HALLIDAY (Harlequins)	17	**D.S. WYLLIE** (Stewarts Melville F.P.)
C.D. MORRIS (Orrell)	18	**G.H. OLIVER** (Hawick)
P.A.G. RENDALL (Wasps)	19	**G.R. MARSHALL** (Selkirk)
C.J. OLVER (Northampton)	20	**D.F. MILNE** (Heriot's F.P.)
M.G. SKINNER (Harlequins)	21	**J.A. HAY** (Hawick)

REFEREE: **S.R. Hilditch (Ireland)**

England 21   Scotland 12

SCORERS

Try Heslop

Conversion Hodgkinson

Penalties: Hodgkinson (5)

SCORERS

Penalties Chalmers (4)

Revenge was sweet for England. The defeat by Scotland the year before had hurt deeply. The pain was caused not so much by a feeling of having been robbed on the day but rather by annoyance that their season's performances had merited some historical accolade. As it was Scotland had beaten them, won the Grand Slam and England's dazzling defeats of France and Wales were no more than fast-fading memories. More than anything else the Murrayfield 1990 defeat shaped England's 1991 campaign. They were not going to be denied again. As a result, victory become their overriding concern. Their game was stripped of any adornment. They played the percentages relying on the power and ability of their pack to win possession and make ground. It worked and one could only admire the single-mindedness of it all. Beauty was in the eye of the beholder and not many England supporters left Twickenham unhappy on this particular afternoon.

Scotland were simply unable to match England in the line-out at which Ackford and Dooley confirmed their status as the best second-row partnership in the world. Heslop's try stemmed from one of the rare moments when England won quick second-phase ball in the Scottish 22. Once again Hodgkinson was a dominant influence, missing only one of seven kicks at goal. The full-back also came into the line beautifully to help set up England's only try. The chief architect of the English victory however was Andrew whose kicking from hand kept Scotland on the turn throughout the match. Well might the England forwards have shaken his hand after the game.

MORE QUALITY THAN YOU
MAY EVER NEED

W e had a score to settle. 13-7 to be precise. That was the margin of defeat last year at Murrayfield in the game which denied us the Grand Slam. The scoreboard said it all: they won, we lost. And it hurt like hell. We were desperate for revenge.

We had a month between the games, just as we had had before our last meeting with Scotland. It can work to your advantage if you have a few injuries to clear up, but usually you prefer to keep things on the boil. You have to miss one of the Five Nations weekends and I am sure that there is no ideal time: it depends on your situation. This year the break did us no favours at all. I took a Saturday off and watched the first half of Scotland demolishing Wales on television before moving on to Wasps to watch the second half of a friendly against Sale. I thought the rest might do me some good. I had played a lot of rugby up to Christmas and had just come through a tough cup-tie against Leicester following our win in Wales. That was to be the last rugby I played until I stepped out at Twickenham to face Scotland.

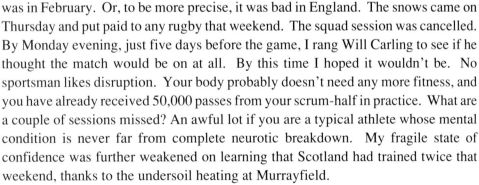

It is still a shock when the weather is really bad in England. Despite countless winters spent skating across frozen pitches, or ploughing through mud, you never quite expect it to be too bad. It was in February. Or, to be more precise, it was bad in England. The snows came on Thursday and put paid to any rugby that weekend. The squad session was cancelled. By Monday evening, just five days before the game, I rang Will Carling to see if he thought the match would be on at all. By this time I hoped it wouldn't be. No sportsman likes disruption. Your body probably doesn't need any more fitness, and you have already received 50,000 passes from your scrum-half in practice. What are a couple of sessions missed? An awful lot if you are a typical athlete whose mental condition is never far from complete neurotic breakdown. My fragile state of confidence was further weakened on learning that Scotland had trained twice that weekend, thanks to the undersoil heating at Murrayfield.

The swines, they were going to do it to us again. They had even played an extra game in the Championship and got the bad one out of their system when losing in

Paris on the opening weekend. You can see what defeat the year before had done to us: first in Cardiff where we were in the grip of fear and now again in the build-up to the Scottish match where we felt the fates were against us. Every sportsman is prey to negative thoughts. Luckily for us, these were fears confined to the privacy of a 'phone line.

However training on Wednesday evening did little to soothe the nerves. The backs had to use the 'Quins 2nd team pitch which had about four inches of snow on it. It was untidy, we were not able to go at full pace and got through very little of what we had intended. Meanwhile Geoff Cooke was frantically trying to get us a decent surface to train on the following day. He came up with Bisham Abbey. My heart sank. I knew the surface at Bisham well and it was very slippery. There was a real threat of injury. Was it once again not to be our year?

These gloomy thoughts came at the end of a difficult three-week period. Difficult in that rugby, for all the wrong reasons, had been the last thing written about. The post-match Cardiff issue rumbled on. Will, Brian Moore and myself had met with some of the journalists on the following Monday. They were sympathetic but that was what we expected as we knew them well and the hostility from other journalists was not too big a problem. Relationships with the RFU were however. There had been a long drawn-out saga about the new amateur regulations. They were a mess. No-one knew quite what they meant. As a result there were endless discussions about what was permissible and what was not. The row with the BBC at Cardiff was an example of how muddled everything had become. Then, just when we thought we had sorted out some workable guidelines, along came the argument over Timberland.

I was one of four players – Paul Ackford, Mike Teague and Brian Moore being the others – approached by the American outdoor leisurewear company to appear in an advertisement. As we were not in England kit, it seemed to meet with all the RFU's guidelines. It was placed in the match programme and promptly rejected by the RFU. Quite who was right or wrong did not matter.

The issue was getting out of hand. There had been nothing in the papers for three weeks except rows concerning England players and money. If I had been an ordinary supporter, even I might have come to the conclusion that the England team were all money-grabbers.

The picture was false. That was why I did an interview with Nigel Starmer-Smith for BBC's Sportsnight in which I stated that our sole objective was to play rugby and to win. Everything else was irrelevant. We wanted to concentrate all our energies into rugby, nothing else. All commercial deals were put on ice. That was wen we parted company with the Willis agency.

So by that Wednesday evening things had most definitely not gone smoothly. But do they ever in sport? The mark of a great sportsman or a great side is that they can put all the hassle behind them, block out all external factors and just draw inwards. That was the great, enduring strength of this squad: we had tremendous belief in each other and shared a deep-rooted desire to make our mark in the history books.

By Thursday morning, the little cloud had lifted. Bisham Abbey had laid a new all-weather surface about ten days earlier. It was superb. Just to be able to run flat out after a week of snow and frost gave me a marvellous boost. At heart, most of us are still kids. We enjoy running and playing with a ball. It is easy to forget that pleasure amidst all the fuss and bother of international rugby. It was nice to have it reconfirmed that morning at Bisham.

We were starting from scratch again. The Welsh match seemed to belong to another season. This time there was tension in the air but it was positive tension. The huge fear of losing had gone. We didn't want to lose to this lot but if we did, they would have damn well earned their victory.

We put a lot of thought into the game. We had not done ourselves justice the year before. The reason was simple: we had been too complacent. We had thumped France and then Wales and were under the impression that all we had to do was turn up at Murrayfield to take the Grand Slam. What fools! Sport does not work like that. Not even rugby, which is a reasonably predictable game. We had acted like the naive cricketer who after being in full flow in the evening, seeing the ball like a football on his way to a century, comes in the next morning and, expecting to be able to carry on where he left off, is out second ball. Everything has to be worked for in sport: nothing can be taken for granted.

We had to focus on two things. The first was to get back to basics. We had to play a very specific game against Scotland and attempt to neutralise their strengths. We could not let their back-row get up a head of steam or allow their hard-tackling midfield to knock us back over the gain line. We had to keep them on the turn, and not give them ball to run on to. That was how we had beaten them at Murrayfield in 1988 and how we should have beaten them at Twickenham in 1989 if, between us, Jon Webb and I had not missed seven kicks at goal.

The second factor was again our attitude. The danger here was that we would get too wound-up. We were determined to put the record right but if we sacrificed control in the cause of passion, then we would be in trouble. I was guilty early in my career of getting too excited. It is a weakness in anyone but for a fly-half it is fatal. A stand-off has to be detached, to be above the mayhem around him, to be cool enough to weigh up the options and to make the right decisions. I was a madman early on, getting stuck into tackles, running all over the place, chasing every loose ball. It did not do me or the side any good. I like to think I learned from it even if there are still many times when I consciously have to rein myself in during a game.

We spent a fair bit of time during that two-day build-up analysing the opposition. How did we ever cope before the video? The answer is that of course we did. But as everyone else now uses the facility, you have to do likewise. There is no doubt that if you have done your homework thoroughly it will give you an advantage. Defences are so well organised now that you have to be able to take advantage of the slightest crack. If you can exert pressure in a certain area, then you might be able to induce that crack yourselves rather than just wait for it to happen.

All players have weaknesses. The video helps you to spot them. We discovered that Craig Chalmers tends to run from one side of the field and pass from another; that Gary Armstrong now kicks off the base of set-pieces more often; that the Scots and Irish chase kicks in a different way to the English. I personally discovered that my defensive kicking was too slow simply because the video showed me that I was taking two paces rather than doing it all in one movement. With all this scientific input, I can hear the romantics screaming: 'Whatever happened to flair?' The simple reply is that there has first to be some sort of collective discipline if flair is to have any chance to come through. I myself used to be a bit sceptical about all this video preparation, but I have now come to appreciate the great benefit it affords. In times past we would just watch whole games on video – half before dinner, half afterwards – often dozing off towards the end. Now we have sequences edited together from several games. It is fascinating stuff – even the video nasties, compilations of all our mistakes. They are not pretty viewing, but very important.

Rugby has progressed so much recently. I am sure everyone who has played the game down the years has felt that he has helped moved the game on a bit. But I do genuinely feel that in my playing career I have seen enormous advances in the approach to the game. It is even different to when I started out. The latest innovation is sports psychology. England dabbled in this scientific approach last season when a guy called Dave Collins had a few sessions with us. Geoff Cooke tried to move it on a little this season by preparing individual tapes for us.

Geoff, through his work as chief executive of the British Institute of Sports

'Long arm of the law' Ackford arrests the ball in mid-flight to the dismay of Cronin and Gray.

Coaches, has had a lot of experience of sports psychology. It is fairly common practice in many sports for the athletes to consider the psychological element in their training. In rugby, it is unheard of. We all sprint to ten in the changing room, utter a few oaths about murdering the opposition and that is about it. Geoff introduced us to the concepts of visualisation, concentration, goal-setting, positive thinking and so on. It was very interesting. However I, and most of the squad, did not really take to it. Perhaps this was just an Englishman's natural scepticism of things new or more likely a typical rugby player's natural aversion to gimmicks. We felt we were already doing many of these things, visualising the perfect kick to trap the full-back or even the diving try in the corner – fantasy, of course, in my case. However I remained a sceptic. It is all very well psyching yourself into a very positive frame of mind. No argument there. But what about when it goes wrong? What about the opposition flanker who refuses to give you that little bit of space to make the break? Surely adaptability is the key element: being able to think on your feet and react to what is going on around you?

It was not the first time I had come across it all. I had played for the Gordon club in Sydney back in 1986. We had a terrible season. In came the sports psychologist for three weeks and lo and behold we won our last three games. It can work for some and not for others. Certainly I can see great benefits for individually-based sports such as athletics where self-belief is instrumental to performance. How else does a pole-vaulter get over the bar if he doesn't believe that he will? But in rugby, who knows? Maybe in ten years time we will see it as the norm. In many ways a good captain or coach already does the job himself only it is not quite so formalised. Certainly doing 64 concentration exercises a day is not for me. For others, maybe; for me, no. I just feel that if I am not strong-willed enough to cope with the ebb and flow of a game then I might as well give up.

Also my efficiency or otherwise depends so much on the performance of those around me. If Richard Hill has an off day, or Paul Ackford can't get off the ground in the line-out, then no matter what positive thoughts I might have in my head, I've got no chance.

How you feel about the people around you is possibly the most important factor of all. No amount of psychological tinkering can hide a weakness. If your hooker, scrum-half, fly-half or whoever is a clown, then you are lumbered with it. In this England side there were no real weaknesses. We could play any game we wanted. During 1990 the ball had flowed. This year it was staying tight. The truth of the matter had been revealed on the field, not in some psychologist's tape. That Thursday evening I felt confident. That sense of hardness, detected in the build-up to the Welsh match but channelled in the wrong direction, was returning. This time it was a more wholesome expression. Even the little upset on Friday morning over a Red Noses stunt could not upset it.

Alan Black at the RFU had fixed up for us to do a photo session with Ma Boswell from the BBC series 'Bread'. A good idea: trouble was no-one had told us. So come training at Bisham Abbey on Friday morning, a venue we had opted for in preference to a rocky surface at The Stoop, we had another mini-confrontation on our hands. In truth it was a storm in a tea-cup. None of us objects to doing charity work. We have done a lot of it over the years without any fuss or favour. Comic Relief was not the issue. The media was. Could we trust them? We had all learnt from Murrayfield 1990, and even prior to that, in 1989, Finlay Calder had told me how much of a boost he got from reading the English media on England's chances. So, what if we wore the red noses? Might the headline say on Saturday morning: 'England Think Scotland Are Clowns'? 'Red Noses for England: Red Faces for Scotland'? The possibilities were endless. In the end we did it. Even so most of the papers reported that there was an almighty argument about us doing it but never examined the reasons why. I am still not quite clear why there should have been a Red Nose photo session then, a full month before the actual Comic Relief Day.

That sort of incident, the day before the Welsh game, might have fazed us. Here it was a minor irritant, soon forgotten. We were in a better frame of mind altogether, looking forward to the contest as any sportsman would, rather than being crippled by the fear of failure. On Friday afternoon we were back at the Petersham Hotel in Richmond. Again, killing time is the problem. We all have different ways of coping with it. If anything, it is more difficult at home games where you have minimal travelling time.

Saturday morning: breakfast, read all those papers avidly that we profess never to read – forwards in one room, backs in another – clean the boots, cup of coffee, maybe a sandwich, final team meeting at 1:00, no need to say much really, it's all so obvious, and on to the bus. In the dressing room, Dean and Rory slump down and read the programme. Brian and 'Winters' are already half-changed and on the couch for a rub down, the hypochondriacs, which means most of us, are putting tape and bandage on those parts which have no need of it but which we once strapped five years ago and so think it still helps. A final word, the mood is good and out to face Scotland.

The match went well for us, the early penalties settling any nerves and confirming that we had the weaponry to succeed. Play it in their half and the pressure would tell. We should perhaps have wrapped up the match before we did, but they came back, or we let them back depending on your perspective of things – whether you are English or Scottish. The score closed to 15-12 and the pressure was back on. We were in a strong frame of mind however. Two more penalties and we were home.

The dressing-room was a good place to be. Looking back it was the happiest of all the four games. By the time the French game came round we were just too drained to whoop it up afterwards. It was not just the understandably sweet joy of revenge which was in the air after Scotland. We had beaten a good side and that enhanced our own status. They were Grand Slam champions and had had a good tour to New Zealand. It was satisfying to know that we had found a way to beat them. This was a triumph for good preparation. Scotland had been a bit of a bogey side, but we

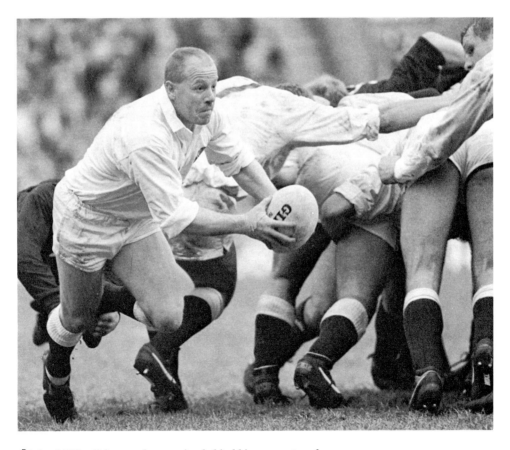

Richard Hill relishes good possession behind his rampant pack.

had worked out how to get the better of them. Keep them on the turn. I had been pleased with my own game, particularly my kicking. I was given a comforting range of options however by the forwards who were winning not only their own ball but Scotland's as well. That meant I could kick the ball off the park, knowing that we had a good chance of stealing their throw. Normally, you only grudgingly concede the throw to the opposition. The referee, Stephen Hilditch, helped us in this aspect. Home Union refs are much better at affording protection to line-out jumpers as well as keeping a sharp eye on offsides. We have a good set-piece side. If I were the opposition, my game plan would be to disrupt as much as possible. Some refs, notably from France and the Southern Hemisphere, are happier than others to let this go on. Fair enough for the opposition if they can get away with it.

We were on course. Not that you would have thought so to judge by some of the criticisms. It is not that we are averse to criticism. We are not. Even Geoff Cooke wondered whether we had not been too inhibited. But at least he was prepared to acknowledge that we were the men on the ground and therefore the ones to make the decisions. He accepted that Scotland had come back into the game and that we felt the need to keep the pressure on. If we are criticised for playing a tight game when our better option would have been to spread it wide, then fair enough. If we are criticised for poor execution of a tight policy rather than merely for choosing that strategy, then fair enough. But to criticise tight play just because it is prettier to watch backs running with the ball, is plain daft. Rugby is a complex sport. Just because the rolling maul looks like a mass of bodies does not mean that it is not a very skilful operation. It most certainly is. Just because a toddler of three can kick a ball, does not mean that it is an easy thing to do. It is not. It is a very precise art. It takes hours and hours of practice. Against Scotland and France it went well for me. Against Wales and Ireland it didn't. A critic should be able to appreciate fully what he is witnessing. Too many of the comments were uninformed and showed lack of understanding.

Perhaps the gloom merchants have been encouraged to expect too much in recent years on account of some very lop-sided games in international rugby. New Zealand hammering Wales; England walloping France in Paris; big wins for various countries against Romania, Fiji and Argentina. These are not true indicators. International rugby is tough and victories have to be earned the hard way. Look back to the Fifties and Sixties and consider some of the scorelines. I am sure there are many ex-internationals, now playing on the great rugby pitch in the sky, who would have been quite happy to have defeated Scotland 21-12. We most certainly were.

Rory Underwood explains to Moore, 'Sorry, Alex, I don't get many chances to run with the ball so I have to make the most of them.'

Engand had a month off. I had a week off. The Scottish match was not for another four weeks, so I had booked a 7-day skiing trip commencing the day after Leicester's game against Wasps. I was looking forward to it. The only slight problem was that I had neglected to tell England about it. A few days before I left I rang Twickenham and left a message to tell them that I would be away. I heard nothing back so I assumed it was alright. I missed a training session the weekend I got back but Geoff Cooke's only comment was that he was relieved I had not broken anything.

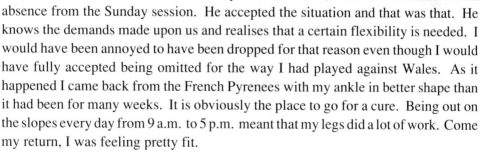

I know full well that some people might have been upset by me going off in the middle of the Five Nations. My only response is that you can't have it every way. That is the only week's holiday I shall have with my wife this year. The rest of my police leave goes on rugby. Add to that the fact that a lot of opportunities for overtime are also sacrificed, and you have a fairly hefty commitment to rugby. You owe your family something. Of course I could have broken my leg. I could also have broken it playing 5-a-side football. Geoff, to his great credit, made no fuss. I was delayed on the return, hence the absence from the Sunday session. He accepted the situation and that was that. He knows the demands made upon us and realises that a certain flexibility is needed. I would have been annoyed to have been dropped for that reason even though I would have fully accepted being omitted for the way I had played against Wales. As it happened I came back from the French Pyrenees with my ankle in better shape than it had been for many weeks. It is obviously the place to go for a cure. Being out on the slopes every day from 9 a.m. to 5 p.m. meant that my legs did a lot of work. Come my return, I was feeling pretty fit.

It was just as well given that the snows arrived in England a few days later. Luckily I played for the police up in Liverpool on the Wednesday which meant that I got a game more than most Englishmen that week. But that was all I played until we ran out at Twickenham. It suits me much better to play rather than to train but the conditions were against us.

Work was fairly debilitating at the time for the simple reason that I was on night shifts. They really sap your energy. No doubt about it, your body clock takes a while to recover. I enjoy my work. I am based at Hinckley Police Station and am assigned to the fast response unit. The job brings you back down to earth. No more the all-conquering Grand Slam hero as you get a kicking in town on a Saturday night. Shift work is hard but it is rewarding. You work closely with the other guys on the shift and you soon build up a close relationship. It is very like rugby in one sense: you depend on them for back-up. No-one lets the other one down. They have been brilliant in the amount of support and cover they have provided just so that I can play rugby. You feel guilty when you return to work, feeling that you have missed out on something, that they have taken all the stick for you. I would not like to be in the position of Will Carling who is constantly at the beck and call of the media. His whole life is rugby and that is not for me. I play it but I don't eat, sleep and drink it. Rugby is a hobby and that is the way, for me anyway, that it should stay.

By the time we met up for the Scotland match, I was feeling quite good. Although not perhaps in top shape, the injuries were at least beginning to clear up. Everyone else was worried that the Scots had sneaked in a couple of training sessions at the weekend but it didn't concern me too much. Come the day, the game would still have to be won. I had seen an awful lot of guys who looked great in training but who never performed in the game.

There was a very determined mood about, a sense that we owed Scotland a hiding after the year before. I had not played in that match so the feeling was not quite as acute with me. Mind you, I am always for giving any side a good hiding, no matter who they are. That is what every game is about. In fact I had never lost to Scotland and as far as I was concerned I was not about to.

We discussed three main things amongst the forwards. The first was the verbal intimidation which had gone on at Murrayfield in 1990 and even the year before that at Twickenham. There had been a lot of shouting and abuse which is mere gamesmanship. The response was simple – do nothing. If they started having a go again it was obvious that they were afraid of us and wanted to put us out of our stride. We also had to stop their forwards getting into positions where they could drive low and hard, as they had done so effectively in New Zealand. That meant a wrap-around tackle was no good. They had to go down and backwards. Finally we targeted Gary Armstrong as a key man. He had improved each year as a player and was very strong around the fringes. Mike Teague was just the man to stop him. If he could do that

A moment of concern as Simon Hodgkinson receives attention to his goal-kicking leg.

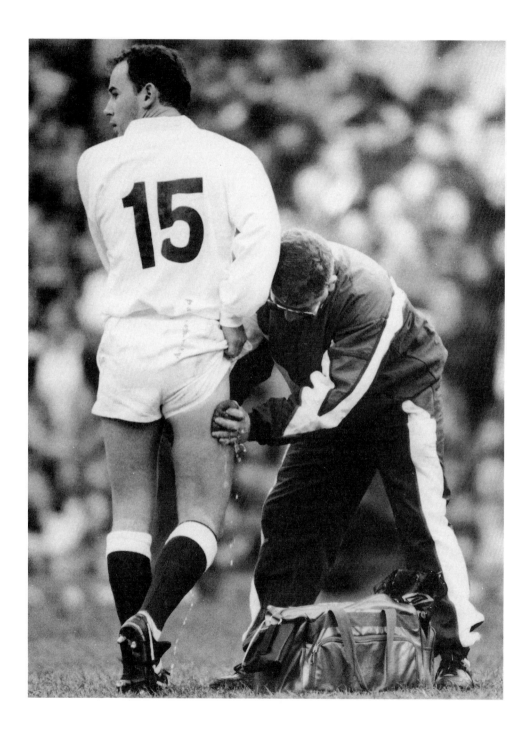

then we knew that Craig Chalmers under pressure was much less of a threat.

When I checked into the Petersham that Wednesday evening there was a formal invitation waiting for me. I opened it:

'Dear Dean. The England forwards invite you to attend a full scrummaging session. A scrummage takes place when the scrum-half puts the ball into the tunnel and lasts until the ball has come out behind the number 8's feet. We do hope you will be able to make it. Casual dress.'

For a long time I have taken stick for my tendency to pop my head out of a scrum to see what's going on. I have got calluses on my hands, according to Paul Ackford, from leaning on so much, whilst some of the other blokes call me 'Ben Hur' given the position I assume on my chariot. My only defence is that we have such a superbly drilled front five that I can afford to be a bit flexible. Give them praise and they tend to shut up. We did have some work to do on the scrummage though. It had not gone that well against Wales. We never put them under pressure. Nevertheless we were never in any trouble, apart from one scrum where they drove us back. To judge by the celebrations you would have thought they had won the match. Scotland had shown what we ought to have done to them. We worked hard that Wednesday evening: binding, feet positions, hand grip, timing, bending and driving. If we wanted to use our back-row to get them on the turn, then we had to have a steady srum.

The line-out too came in for a lot of attention over those two days. Again we intended to cut them. We had studied Chris Gray in particular and noticed that he never really jumped on the opposition ball but faced inwards and drove. In a two man line-out this tactic would be rendered invalid as well as exposed to the referee.

Jeremy Guscott spoils one of the few chances Gavin Hastings had to attack.

The two days flew by, probably because the training itself was

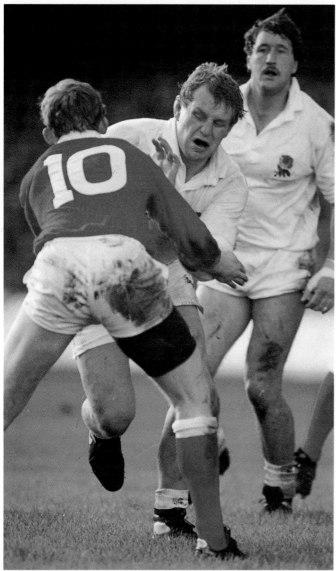

Wales 6   England 25

ABOVE *Brian Moore has his own greeting for the television audience.*
TOP *Mike Teague crashes over for England's only try.*
LEFT *Neil Jenkins has the daunting task of dealing with Dean Richards. Mike Teague stands by in support.*

FOLLOWING PAGE *Wade Dooley, Brian Moore and Jeff Probyn move in as Mark Ring goes down with the ball.*

England 21   Scotland 12

ABOVE *John Jeffrey manages to get the ball away under pressure from Mike Teague.*
RIGHT *Nigel Heslop and Simon Hodgkinson enjoy Twickenham success against the Scots.*
FACING PAGE *Derek White gains impressive height to win the line-out. Gary Armstrong waits below.*

Ireland 7 England 16
ABOVE LEFT *Nowhere to go
for Keith Crossan.*
LEFT *Brendan Mullin leaps to catch
the ball, but is caught himself by
Jeremy Guscott and Will Carling.*

ABOVE *Rob Andrew on the burst with Will Carling in support.*
LEFT *Joy for try-scorer Mike Teague. Nigel Heslop and Peter Winterbottom also enjoy the moment as England's pressure finally seals the fate of the Irish in injury time.*

Cathay Pacific.
The foremost exponents of non-stop flight.

LEFT *Building strength for the final showdown.*
BOTTOM LEFT *Roger Uttley in discussion with the England pack.*
BELOW *Working together – Geoff Cooke and Will Carling.*
BOTTOM *Mike Teague relieves the pre-match tension with Peter Winterbottom, Wade Dooley, Paul Ackford and Dean Richards.*

England 21 France 19

ABOVE *Grand Slam hopefuls – the
England team line up for the cameras
before the match against France. Back
row (left to right): D. Bevan (touch
judge), G. Cooke (manager),
S.J. Halliday, J.M. Webb,
R. Underwood, P.J. Winterbottom,
M.C. Teague, P.J. Ackford,
W.A. Dooley, D. Richards,
J.A. Probyn, J. Leonard, M.G. Skinner,
C.D. Morris, R.M. Uttley (coach),
C. Norling (touch judge). Front row:
P.A.G. Rendall, N.J. Heslop,
B.C. Moore, R.J. Hill, W.D.C. Carling
(captain), C.R. Andrew, J.C. Guscott,
S. Hodgkinson, C.J. Olver.*
RIGHT *Philippe Saint-André scores
France's memorable first try.*
FAR RIGHT *Rory Underwood scores
England's try to the delight of the
supporters in the South Stand.*

FOLLOWING PAGE *Jeff Probyn shows
the strain of life as a prop forward.*

LEFT *Grand Slam! The moment of victory.*
BELOW *Champagne celebrations under the West Stand.*

fairly concentrated as well as the fact that we had to make an hour and a half coach ride back and forth to Bisham Abbey. In between times it was on to the cribbage table with Jerry Guscott. There used to be a flourishing bridge school when Stuart Barnes was involved, not to mention a few trips to the casino. For my part I would be much happier to get out of bed on a Saturday morning and play the game then and there. Like most of the players, I don't enjoy the hanging around.

I get slightly nervous before a game but nothing untoward. I think it is more impatience at wanting to get on with it. By the time we got out on to the pitch against Scotland I was ready for action. They were not. You could see it in their faces. They were looking around during the anthems, and even early in the game they would not look you in the eye. I know it can be a trite thing to believe that you can see it in the eyes, but you generally can. Watching the video of last year's Grand Slam match you could see the Scots

'Hey ref, any chance of you standing between me and Gary Armstrong for a couple of minutes.'

were hell-bent on victory, faces set in stone from the moment they came out of the tunnel. This year they played with great vigour but they didn't really have it deep down. It may only be a thin line between playing with vigour and playing with passion but it's a crucial one nonetheless.

We stuck to our pattern throughout, providing enough good ball for Rob Andrew to do the business. Even when they closed to 15-12 I wasn't worried and just encouraged the forwards to stick to the plan of sucking them in and driving. I was shattered by the end and slumped in the bath for at least half an hour. Whether it is me getting older or the games faster, I certainly seem more tired at the end these days. I hope it is the latter. Certainly you have to be much fitter to play international rugby than you did even when I first started. A forward like Maurice Colclough, who made even my fitness regime look polished and committed, would no longer last the pace. I am not sure that Wales have got worse in recent years it is just that they have stood still while all the other countries have considerably improved their fitness and general training standards. Everything is so much more thorough from the video analysis to the work on the athletics track.

I found some of the post-match criticism difficult to fathom. Those that said we should entertain more should have canvassed all the supporters leaving Twickenham that afternoon. I am certain that the vast majority were more than satisfied to see us win. Simple as that. And the reason is simple. Most of those spectators have played the game; they know what it is like out there and how easy it is for a game to turn against you.

I was not too concerned by this line of criticism. I was, however, put out by some of David Sole's comments. Although he may have been misquoted or misrepresented, he was reported as saying that we had been boring and that Jeff Probyn, his opposite number, had been guilty of dangerous play. What he said was no more than sour grapes and I would not have expected this from him. Jeff had

beaten him fair and square in the scrummage and he should have been able to face up to that. Moaning about it did him no good. Once the game is over, that should be that.

All in all we were happy, particularly up front. If some folk were moaning that England were playing too tight, it had to mean that the forwards were going well. The criticism was in fact a compliment.

Played two, won two, two to go.

The
Triple Crown

Lansdowne Road, Dublin
Saturday 2nd March

IRELAND 7 ENGLAND 16

Ireland England

Ireland		England
J.E. STAPLES London Irish	15	**S.D. HODGKINSON** Nottingham
S.P. GEOGHEGAN London Irish	14	**N.J. HESLOP** Orrell
B.J. MULLIN Blackrock College	13	**W.D.C. CARLING (captain)** Harlequins
D.M. CURTIS London Irish	12	**J.C. GUSCOTT** Bath
K.D. CROSSAN Instonians	11	**R. UNDERWOOD** Leicester
B.A. SMITH Leicester	10	**C.R. ANDREW** Wasps
R. SAUNDERS (captain) London Irish	9	**R.J. HILL** Bath
J.J. FITZGERALD Young Munster	1	**J. LEONARD** Harlequins
S.J. SMITH Ballymena	2	**B.C. MOORE** Harlequins
D.C. FITZGERALD Lansdowne	3	**J.A. PROBYN** Wasps
B.J. RIGNEY Greystones	4	**P.J. ACKFORD** Harlequins
N.P.J. FRANCIS Blackrock College	5	**W.A. DOOLEY** Preston Grasshoppers
P.M. MATTHEWS Wanderers	6	**M.C. TEAGUE** Gloucester
G.F. HAMILTON N.I.F.C.	7	**P.J. WINTERBOTTOM** Harlequins
B.F. ROBINSON Ballymena	8	**D. RICHARDS** Leicester

REPLACEMENTS		REPLACEMENTS
K.J. MURPHY (Cork Constitution)	16	**J.M. WEBB** (Bath)
V.J.G. CUNNINGHAM (St Mary's)	17	**S.J. HALLIDAY** (Harlequins)
A.C. ROLLAND (Blackrock College)	18	**C.D. MORRIS** (Orrell)
N.P. MANNION (Lansdowne)	19	**P.A.G. RENDALL** (Wasps)
G.F. HALPIN (Wanderers)	20	**C.J. OLVER** (Northampton)
T.J. KINGSTON (Dolphin)	21	**M.G. SKINNER** (Harlequins)

REFEREE: **A. Ceccon (France)**

Ireland 7 England 16

SCORERS

Try Geoghegan

Penalty Smith (B)

SCORERS

Tries Underwood, Teague

Conversion Hodgkinson

Penalties Hodgkinson (2)

Many thought this would be England's toughest match. So it proved. Ireland did not concede the lead until seven minutes from the end. It took a moment of brilliance from Rory Underwood to edge England in front and on the way to their first Triple Crown for 11 years. It was Underwood's 26th international try and, on his own admission, 'the most important'. When he received the ball on the Irish 22 there seemed little on. He was surrounded by a gaggle of would-be Irish tacklers. Underwood went up on his toes, slid inside one tackle, outside another and he was clear, roared on as much by his relieved team-mates as the thousands of English supporters who had crossed the Irish Sea. England were only three points to the good but that audacious try knocked the heart out of the Irish. Teague plundered a close-range try in the closing moments and Hodgkinson's difficult conversion sent him to an England record points total of 46 for the Championship. This beat by two points Dusty Hare's tally, achieved seven years earlier. The Nottingham full-back was not quite on his mettle however, missing four kicks at goal during the match. The English plaudits really belonged to the pack and to Richards in particular. As his side struggled to come to terms with the battling fury of the Irish, the Leicester number 8 slowly pulled the match his and England's way. He was a huge force in the loose, won ball at the tail of the line-out and was a crucial link in the Underwood try. Geoghegan was in irrepressible form for Ireland, his try just after half-time was a gem of pace and balance as he swerved through Underwood's tackle. The Irish winger's exuberance typified the spirit and wit with which the Irish played the game. England were mightily relieved to hear the final whistle. The Triple Crown was theirs and the Grand Slam beckoned.

1992
CATHAY PACIFIC
HongKongBank
INVITATION SEVENS

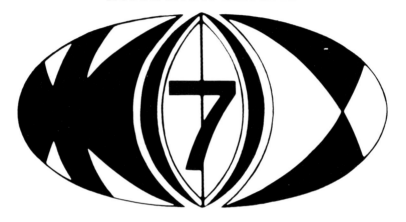

Hong Kong Government Stadium
April 4th and 5th 1992

For more information please ring
071-839 2622

CATHAY PACIFIC
Arrive in better shape.

There is no rest during the Five Nations. Even if you are not captain of your club, as I am at Wasps, then you still have a huge responsibility to the guys you play with week in, week out. To them a league or a cup match is every bit as important as the Calcutta Cup or the Triple Crown. It's all relative.

At Wasps there was little respite. After the high of beating Scotland, came the low of being knocked out of the cup by Orrell. I felt the disappointment keenly but at least had the massive compensation of playing for England. In fact, I had no time to dwell on the cup defeat for, as I soon as I had done a fairly lengthy interview for BBC's Grandstand, cramped in the corner of a noisy Wasps' clubhouse, it was straight down to the Petersham Hotel for England training. 'Oh, hello, Dewi Morris and Nigel Heslop. How did you get on this afternoon. Knocked Wasps out of the cup, did you ? How nice for you.'

Yes, it's like that, I am afraid. You can't even moan to the other guys that you were robbed as your tormentors are sitting in the chair next to you. It was the same before the French match. We went to Bath in the league and beat them, their first-ever home defeat in the league. Who do I room with? Richard Hill. There really is no place to hide. It is often assumed that playing against England colleagues must be difficult. Quite the opposite. There is a very good sporting air to the exchanges, competitive but always tinged with respect. It is the way sport should be played: hard, but when it's over, you shake hands and have a drink. I suppose going to bed with your opponent on a Saturday night, as I do with Richard Hill, may be taking cordiality a bit far!

The fixtures programme is cluttered and could do with sorting out. Perhaps the Five Nations could be played a little later in the year but I hear that France have objections to this because it would conflict with the final stages of their club championship. Whatever, there is no doubt that I could have done without playing Bath the week before taking on France. By this time of the season your body, as well as your mind, can only take so much more. At club training during this period I don't do any fitness. Your body needs rest rather than work. In fact playing for Wasps is more disjointed than playing for England. I have played with the same 15 blokes for England all season, but have rarely done that four weeks in a row with Wasps. Consequently most of our training is centred around organising the side – the moves, the strategy, the tactics – as opposed to the old system of fifty laps of the pitch followed by some GBH on the tackle bags. Those days are gone. Fitness work is done in your own time and the whole approach is far more scientific.

England training has changed as well, even within the last few years. Quite apart from the advances with sports psychology and videos, the whole emphasis has altered. This is primarily because we have a settled side. In the bad old days, England sessions on Thursday and Friday were spent desperately trying to pull the strands together in time for Saturday's game. Now we can take it one stage further. We can analyse the opposition and work our strategy around that. There is far more discussion about things. Before, it was almost a monologue with the coach giving his version and everyone too afraid to raise any objections lest he be dropped for the next game. It was a coach's team that took the field in those days: now it is *our* team. It belongs to the players. For that, massive credit must go to Geoff Cooke. He pledged his faith in us, and in no-one more than me, and it has paid off. We believe in ourselves because we know he believes in us. If we fail then we know it is because we really were not good enough. No other excuses are now possible.

Ireland was sure to be another tough test. The games had fallen well for us. Ireland was the Triple Crown match. We could focus on that, a massive achievement in itself, and not make the mistake of last year, get carried away by it all and start thinking too soon about the Grand Slam. Our sights were firmly set on Dublin. If it went well, great, then we could target France. If it went badly...we don't think about that sort of thing. Well, only in Cardiff. And for much of the second half in Dublin as it transpired.

Some people thought prior to the Championship that Ireland would be our toughest test. So it proved. We were on a bit of a roll having come through, in different ways, two difficult tests. In theory there was a slight danger of complacency. In practice however the lure of the Triple Crown put paid to that potential concern. That and the trouble Ireland had caused France in their opening match in Dublin. It was a new side and a very promising one. We had to be on our mettle.

Once again, away from home. But what a contrast in atmosphere. That opening match in Wales had been an ordeal, almost entirely of our own making I must add. Now we were looking forward to travelling to Dublin, a tremendous place whenever and whyever you go; we were looking forward to pitting ourselves against Ireland, freed somewhat from the ogre of defeat which had so frightened us in Cardiff; and we were looking forward to that first crock of gold, the Triple Crown, if we reached the end of the rainbow. Victory is always important to any sportsman at any level. Why else play if it is not to win? Sure, it is fun, but most of that fun, for me at least, comes from winning. It doesn't mean that you can't take defeat. You can, but it hurts, make no mistake.

Victory over Ireland would establish us as the best of the Home Unions, a milestone we had not passed for 11 years. That is an important achievement, not just in itself, but also because you know the opposition so much better: you meet them all the time, on the field, socially, through the press columns if you like, which means that defeat is that much harder to stomach. It is far more personal than losing to France for example.

Life is a rush at this stage of the season. I am lucky that I live only twenty minutes away from Richmond, and only about five minutes from Wasps in north London. My travelling time is kept to a minimum. How the other guys manage I don't know. What with that and work as well. In the build-up to an international you have to cram five days work into three. For those that spend Wednesday travelling down to London, the week is even more condensed. No-one likes to ask too many favours from work-mates, no matter how obliging they are. You feel awkward about it. By the time you have battled through the three-day workload, you are relieved to get away to join England. Much of the benefit of meeting up on a Wednesday is that it gives you time to wind down from work, put all those problems out of your mind. Mind you, by the time you have been put through the treadmill of international rugby, you are mighty glad to get back to work on a Monday. A change is as good as a rest.

Rest was the last thing we got in the build-up to Ireland. Geoff Cooke was away on business so Mike Slemen, the 'B' coach, took both the Sunday and Wednesday evening sessions with the backs. A new face, a few new ideas, a few new drills, it's all good stuff. It is very easy to become stale, even at this level, when you are used to the players around you and the coach in front of you. All you really want to do is get on with the match.

Mike kept us on our toes, and that was an achievement in itself given the atrocious weather on the Wednesday. It poured down, we were on the second team pitch again at the 'Quins ground, The Stoop, and we ploughed through the mud. Nothing like acclimatising for Dublin weather and conditions, we thought. How right we were.

Thursday was hectic. Video at 9 o'clock, training at 10, hotel at noon, pack, lunch and on the bus to Heathrow at 1 p.m. Dublin at 5:30, Fitzpatrick castle, Kiliney, south Dublin at 7 that evening and we were shattered. Still, that is all part of the challenge of playing away from home. In fact, you can't win. As already mentioned, at home you find the time drags, whereas away, you are on the move the whole time.

However that Thursday evening, things were not quite right. Perhaps it was the rush, perhaps it was because Geoff had only joined us at Heathrow, perhaps it was a touch of complacency creeping in. However we had not been as sharp as we ought to have been. So, after dinner we held an impromptu team meeting. No management, no coaches, just the players. It was the only one of its kind we held that season. Not to clear the air or anything, because there were few secrets or sly whispers amongst this squad. The aim was to set the tone once more, get people back on their toes. It was not a simple case of Will giving us a rollicking: that would have done little good. It had to come from within us. The great thing about this bunch of players is that everyone has a say and there will be conflicting points of view. I felt that we were not sharp enough in training; Paul Ackford disagreed. It didn't matter who was right. The discussion focused our minds.

All through the season we kept assessing our mental approach, not in any formal or even crank-psychologist way, but just by gauging the attitude to training, the input from the players and the mood before the games. A lot of the appraisal is of course guesswork. Who really knows whether a game will go your way? The best England training session in which I have ever participated was at Peebles last year, the day before we played Scotland for the Grand Slam. Look what happened then. Our preoccupation with getting in the right frame of mind, whatever that might be, stemmed from that game. It was only afterwards that we saw the error of our ways. The guys on the bench such as John Olver and Mark Bailey, remarked on it. We were just too relaxed. Hindsight is always a great tutor, but after that we just made sure that everyone was tuned in to the job ahead. That doesn't mean that you can't have a laugh and a joke before the game. Not at all: false seriousness would probably be a bigger obstacle to success than anything. Thursday evening set us up well.

Friday's session at Blackrock College was sharp, slick but utterly useless in preparing us for the conditions which prevailed the next day. It was a sunny, warm, spring morning. By Saturday afternoon the Dublin gods had dumped a load of their messiest weather all over the city. However, it felt good that morning, not just in what we did, but to be in Dublin, to be at Blackrock College with their lovely ladies who fuss over us with their tea, sandwiches and cakes after training. Even if they have

TOP *Dean Richards on the rampage, taking advantage of England's forward superiority.*
ABOVE *Brian Smith clears to touch under extreme pressure from Wade Dooley.*

demolished the lovely old clubhouse, literally a fine old Georgian house, to make way for more streamlined changing facilities. It is on mornings like this, when you have trained hard and met with gentle, friendly folk, that you count your blessings that you are involved with international rugby.

I went with Simon Hodgkinson to Lansdowne Road to see if we could do some kicking practice together. We could not. No point worrying about groundsmen: they are the same the world over be it rugby, cricket, croquet or whatever. Some of the guys went to watch England 'B' play Ireland. I fancied a quieter afternoon, just grooving myself into the game ahead. By the time Paul Ackford and a few of the others returned from the 'B' match, I was ready for a further kick up the backside to get me fully sharp. The news that England had been soundly beaten was taken in the right way. This will be a tough one.

Only Dublin can lay on the weather it does. Saturday morning was filthy. Still, it did not really worry us. If anything, the Irish would have pulled back their curtains on Saturday morning with more of a heavy heart. It was England who had the pack for a wet weather game. Our backs meeting that morning in Geoff Cooke's room emphasised that: no mistakes, keep it tight and don't set up the midfield where they can be tackled. Otherwise there will be a green tide flowing through. We had hoped to move the ball more in this match simply because we figured it might be to our advantage. However, the rain lashing down outside looked like putting paid to those

plans. We had played Ireland in the wet before, in 1989, and had won 16-3 by playing controlled football. We were comfortable with the idea.

How wrong we were. Eight minutes to go and we trailed 7-6. It was all slipping away. We had failed to subdue the Irish threat. We had aimed for two-man line-outs to take maximum advantage of our big men – Dooley and Ackford. We never tapped or

The crucial try. Before (left) ...and after (right).

tidied well enough from those positions. Our kicking from hand was not as precise as it could have been and, quite simply, Ireland were damn good opponents.

Panic never really set in. Not quite, anyway. For the first and only time that season, there was however an edge to some of the exchanges in the huddle. I missed a drop at goal, so next time I cut back to the forwards who promptly berated me for not dropping at goal. And so it went on. Not for very long but that tremor of anxiety was there all right. Who was that, sitting up on the stand at Lansdowne Road, but that old rogue ghost from Murrayfield 1990. He was there, taunting us. You are going to blow it again. The circumstances were almost identical. An away game, expected to win, similar opponents, the opposition scoring a crucial try just after half-time even in the same corner of the field.

However, we were different. We were harder, more together and altogether more canny than the year before. We might well have lost if the game had been in 1990. This year it was over our dead bodies. We were not going to panic. The game itself was different. We were never more than a score behind and we were creating pressure situations. We had reason to keep cool. Sure enough it came, albeit there didn't look the remotest possibility of a score when Rory received the ball. He did it. Somehow he did it. And the weight of a whole tortured 12 months was suddenly lifted in that glorious moment as he crossed the line. Ireland would not come back from that, I felt sure. The Triple Crown was ours. At last something in the bag.

We had clambered out of a pretty deep hole in that match. No doubt about it. It could have gone away from us. Still, look back to the Grand Slam campaign of 1980 and it is only Welshmen who remember that Billy Beaumont's side won 9-8 in the last minutes, three penalties to two tries. As Bill said at the time, just look at the scoreboard. That is all that counts.

It is funny how, when you look back on a season, little moments of play stick in your mind. Two came from the Ireland

game. The first was Simon Hodgkinson's kick which brought the scores to 7-6. It was his most important kick of the season. We were not making any headway and we badly needed some reward for our pressure. Not just on the scoreboard, but psychologically. It was not an easy kick, half-way out, from the wrong side for a right-footed kicker. But over it went.

The second flashback is of Nigel Heslop pinned in his corner, 15 mad Irishmen closing in for the kill, Lansdowne Road baying for him to be buried, the whole of Ireland on the rampage and Nigel, just inches from the touchline, manages to clear

the ball 60 yards downfield, the ball lands on the exact blade of grass intended, turns at right angles and into touch. What do you mean: did he mean it? Of course he meant it. That set us up for a sequence of two or three line-outs from which Dean and Mike Teague pounded away at their midfield. That softening up process was crucial for it was from that base that Rory was to get away.

It was a happy scene in the dressing-room. There was not much noise because it had been a massively draining game. But we had come through. We had won the Triple Crown and nobody could ever take that away from us. A long night of celebration lay ahead. And Dublin was just the place to do it.

Visible signs of a hard-fought game.

There is not time to step back and really take in what is going on. Once you get into that run of three internationals in a row you have barely time to breathe let alone take stock. If it is not work, it is club training; if it is not England training, it is travelling to England training. If there had been another game after the French one I don't think I would have made it.

Still, our minds were set. If we wanted success, we had to earn it. Not so much in the 80 minutes of the game, but in all the commitment around it. The actual playing is the easy part. We all realised that this was probably our last chance to achieve something. This team would not go on beyond the World Cup. We didn't just want the success for ourselves either. As we had been together such a long time, we had grown very close. The sacrifice of time and energy was worth it simply because of the huge bond you felt with those around you. If they could put up with it, then so could you.

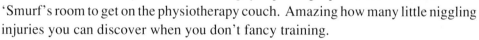

The build-up to the Ireland match showed how the season had already taken its toll. We went through the motions on the Sunday, afraid to take up the offer of cancelling the session just in case we went on to lose. No logic to it: just neurosis. You can measure the level of enthusiasm by the number of guys queuing up outside 'Smurf's room to get on the physiotherapy couch. Amazing how many little niggling injuries you can discover when you don't fancy training.

Wednesday evening was not a whole lot better. It was throwing it down with rain which is not a great help if you are aiming to do a lot of stationary set-piece work. There are guys in the world who actually like training. Or at least those like the All Blacks who get quite psyched up for it and give it whole-hearted commitment. To each their own, I say. Wednesday evening did not do me a lot of good.

What did do me a lot of good was to slip down the road in Dublin on Thursday evening for a couple of pints. Richards, Dooley, Ackford, Teague – a quartet desperate for a break from it all. Dublin was just the place to blow away the cobwebs. We slipped away after dinner, found a nice quiet little pub and had a lovely chat and a drink with the locals. It was a chance to unwind and did all of us more good than

ABOVE AND RIGHT *Heslop, Hodgkinson and Carling take part in the Irish Spot-the-Ball competition.*

any number of lengths on the training field. It is not an approach which would suit everyone and it is not something we have ever done before, but it was the right thing to do that night. As we strolled back Ackers confessed that it had been the best part of the build-up all season. As we sidled in close to midnight we passed Geoff Cooke who was sitting in the hotel bar. I have no idea if he knew where we had been. I have no idea if he cared, 48-hour curfew on alcohol or not. Once again, the mark of the guy is that he trusts us. I dread the day when rugby may be hounded by the tabloid press the way that soccer is. It never crossed my mind that such an incident could ever be of any interest to a newspaper. However on reflection I can see the possibilities and it appals me. Luckily I doubt that rugby will ever attract quite that level of attention. The game is much better without it.

Even though I felt much better after the rest and recreation of the night before, the Friday training session was still a bit of a shambles. By this stage most of the organisation is left in the hands of the forwards. We simply had not given it enough thought. We had not worked out exactly how we wanted to play, who we wanted to target, how we wanted the game to develop or how we were going to control the Irish.

Our sloppy approach almost cost us dear on the day. Everyone was more relaxed than for the previous two games. In part it is the charm of Ireland working on you. The ladies at Blackrock College are famed for their tea, cakes and friendliness. Difficult to envisage that you will be getting hammered by their countrymen in less than 24 hours. I think the real cause of our ragged attitude was tiredness. Simple as that. All teams have to come to terms with it, so it is not an excuse. That is why if you do come through the whole series unbeaten, then it is a massive achievement.

Friday afternoon and over to the great man of the cinema – Brian Moore. His offering this time for the hotel video was that celebrated piece of celluloid, 'The Thief, The Cook, His Wife and Her Lover.' It was a masterpiece, a masterpiece of bad taste. The lounge was cleared in ten minutes, leaving 'Mooro' in piece. Perhaps that was the original intention.

Saturday dawned wet and miserable. Perfect: my kind of weather. Bring the game to me and I am quite happy. Take it to the wide open spaces and the smile soon goes from my face. The conditions suited us but we did not use them to our advantage. Again it was not so much a lack of concentration as a lack of preparation. We were not as fired up as we should have been. You can prepare to counter all of Ireland's

technical shortcomings but you can never adequately prepare for their passion.

In the line-out we knew Neil Francis would be a problem from first-hand experience the previous year. He had cleaned us out at the start of the match at Twickenham. Again we were aiming for the two-man line to neutralise any bumping that might go on. Ireland, we had noted, had played well in the line-out against France, mixing their jumpers well. The scrummage ought to have gone our way. We were far more experienced. However the fire in their belly can make up for any supposed weaknesses, not that there were any in evidence, And so we never came to dominate Ireland. We moved one scrum back in the second half by about four or five yards but that was their only moment of fallibility.

7-6 down and time was running out. If there is one thing I have learned in rugby it is that you play to the whistle. I had recent personal experience of that truism, my old mate Rob Andrew knocking us out of the Cup with an injury time penalty just a few weeks before. Even then Leicester had a chance to snatch it when John Liley, in about the 20th hour of stoppage-time, missed from about 50 yards. With Simon Hodgkinson in the side, we knew it was just a matter of keeping pressure on and the opportunities would come our way. Our forwards were intent on playing 'keep ball' in that last period in an attempt to wear them down and force them into mistakes. I felt that a score would come but did not expect it to come from where it did, out there on the wing. I had envisaged more of a Mike Teague-type try of the sort he eventually scored in the last minute. Nevertheless, all scores gratefully received.

Mike Teague celebrates his second try of the Championship to give England a comfortable winning margin.

Ireland were the hardest opponents of the lot. We sat in the dressing-room with a mixture of emotions – jubilation at having won the Triple Crown, tinged with a sense of horror at how desperately close we had come to losing it. We had taken so long to get going, primarily because they took the game to us. My opposite number, Brian Robinson, had a good match as did most of their forwards. My club mate, Brian Smith, might have made it to the line at one point in the second-half but, I am glad to say, chose to kick. The try we gave away to Simon Geoghegan was a bit tame and exposed our defence. But full credit to him for taking it the way he did. Personally I felt my game was a lot better than it had been in that opener in Cardiff simply because I was lasting the pace. I could still do things in the last 10-15 minutes, which is the critical part of any match, and although I let the Irish full-back Jim Staples past me at one point, I was much happier with my fitness overall.

We were in the history books. It felt quite good, although nothing ever quite sinks in until a lot later. We needed to have some tangible reward because I am not sure that self-belief could have stretched much further if we had lost. Now that we had won, you could already sense a much more positive, confident frame of mind. I had been at it for five years in international rugby and knew that chances to make your mark were few and far between. If you didn't take them when they were offered, as they had been in both 1989 and 1990, then you were a very lucky man if you got another chance. We had been lucky, but I think we had earned it.

The
Grand Slam

Twickenham
Saturday 16th March

ENGLAND 21 FRANCE 19

England France

England		France
S.D. HODGKINSON Nottingham	15	**S. BLANCO (captain)** Biarritz
N.J. HESLOP Orrell	14	**J.-B. LAFOND** Racing Club
W.D.C. CARLING (captain) Harlequins	13	**P. SELLA** Agen
J.C. GUSCOTT Bath	12	**F. MESNEL** Racing Club
R. UNDERWOOD Leicester	11	**P. SAINT-ANDRÉ** Montferrand
C.R. ANDREW Wasps	10	**D. CAMBERABERO** Béziers
R.J. HILL Bath	9	**P. BERBIZIER** Agen
J. LEONARD Harlequins	1	**G. LASCUBÉ** Agen
B.C. MOORE Harlequins	2	**P. MAROCCO** Montferrand
J.A. PROBYN Wasps	3	**P. ONDARTS** Biarritz
P.J. ACKFORD Harlequins	4	**M. TACHDJIAN** Racing Club
W.A. DOOLEY Preston Grasshoppers	5	**O. ROUMAT** Dax
M.C. TEAGUE Gloucester	6	**X. BLOND** Racing Club
P.J. WINTERBOTTOM Harlequins	7	**L. CABANNES** Racing Club
D. RICHARDS Leicester	8	**A. BENAZZI** Agen

REPLACEMENTS		REPLACEMENTS
J.M.WEBB (Bath)	16	**T. LACROIX** (Dax)
S.J. HALLIDAY (Harlequins)	17	**E. BONNEVAL** (Toulouse)
C.D. MORRIS (Orrell)	18	**H. SANZ** (Narbonne)
P.A.G. RENDALL (Wasps)	19	**C. DESLANDES** (Racing Club)
C.J. OLVER (Northampton)	20	**M. CÉCILLON** (Bourgoin)
M.G. SKINNER (Harlequins)	21	**P. GIMBERT** (Bègles)

REFEREE: **L. Peard (Wales)**

England 21

SCORERS

Try Underwood
Conversions Hodgkinson
Penalties Hodgkinson (4)
Drop-goal Andrew

France 19

SCORERS

Tries Saint-André, Camberabero, Mesnel
Conversions Camberabero (2)
Penalty Camberabero

It was a momentous day. The great virtues of the sport were all there: pride, grace, power, athleticism, courage, resilience, patience and, at the end, massive joy. It was by far England's best performance of the season and, to many, their greatest ever afternoon at Twickenham. To come through for their first Grand Slam in 11 years, and, more remarkably, only their third in 63 years, they had to subdue a French side rich in imagination and full of audacity. France scored a try which history will acclaim as one of the best ever. That it did not bring the spoils France's way speaks volumes for the true grit of the England side. The sheer effrontery of the score and the fact that it came so early in the match, the 11th minute, might well have ripped the heart out of most sides. France fielded a failed penalty attempt behind the posts. England turned for the drop out. It was a fatal lapse. Blanco, the incomparable Blanco, was already moving out of defence. First Lafond, then Sella, then Camberabero, a deft chip and catch, a precise cross-kick and just 17 seconds after a near England miss, there was Saint-André diving between the posts. England though were not to be rattled. Underwood crowned a fine season with his 27th international try, Andrew dropped a goal and Hodgkinson, even if he did miss two kicks from in front of the posts, did what he had been doing all season and kicked the goals. France's try from Camberabero owed much to good fortune whilst Mesnel's late effort owed much to great athleticism. It was too late however. The honours belonged to England.

Fast decisions win the game.

Sometimes the difference between winning and losing is a matter of good judgement and split-second timing.

At HongkongBank we know you need fast decisions. Our team is dedicated to helping you seize opportunities as they arise. We have been fully international for more than 125 years, executing game-winning strategies with our strength, experience and speed. We'll help you tackle any problems and reach your own financial goals.

In today's rough and tumble business world, we'll make sure you come out on top.

So make a winning move. Join a team that knows the score. In any field.

HongkongBank

The Hongkong and Shanghai Banking Corporation Limited

Marine Midland Bank • Hang Seng Bank
The British Bank of the Middle East • HongkongBank
of Australia • Hongkong Bank of Canada

Wardley • James Capel • CM&M
Equator Bank

Carlingford and Gibbs Insurance Groups

Fast decisions. Worldwide.

So this was it then. For the second time in two years, we were up for the Grand Slam. Most players don't even get one sniff at it, let alone two. I felt privileged. I felt proud. And I felt at peace with myself.

The hard part is not really in winning the fourth one. That takes care of itself and you can do nothing about it. The hard part is getting into that position in the first place. England had done it two years running, and that was some achievement in itself. To be part of such a successful period in English rugby gave me a huge amount of pleasure. Also, we had proved that last year was no fluke. We had proved in taking the Triple Crown that we were a good side. Now we had to beat France to prove that we were a great side. I was looking forward to it. May the best man win.

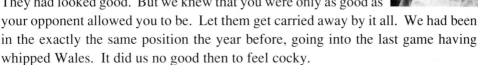

It suited us that France were being considered the best man, particularly after their demolition of Wales in Paris. Fair enough. They had looked good. But we knew that you were only as good as your opponent allowed you to be. Let them get carried away by it all. We had been in the exactly the same position the year before, going into the last game having whipped Wales. It did us no good then to feel cocky.

We also knew that we could get the better of the French. However dazzling they looked, however potent their threequarter line was, we knew that we had the whip hand on them. Stodgy, boring England had more than proved a match in the past for brilliant, free-wheeling France. We had beaten them in Paris in 1990 : we had beaten them 11-0 at Twickenham the year before; and we really ought to have beaten them in 1988, going down narrowly, 10-9. There was no bogey for us to lay here: no fear of the opposition's restrictive game plan to contend with; no *laissez-faire* referee to worry; Les Peard was a good official. Above all there was no fear of failure.

If I could have found the time to contemplate all this, it would have felt rather pleasant. As it was, the days before were the usual mad rush to fulfil commitments; to work, to club, to family, to media, and last of all to your body. It too needs looking after, either some sharp speed work, or light weights in the gym. It was not easy to find the time. The Sunday after an international is a wash-out. It is the toughest day of all in many ways. There is no doubt that your body is still charged with adrenalin, so slumping in an armchair is by no means easy. Your mind too is still buzzing, crackling with all the strain of the pre-match nerves. In contrast to this your limbs are screaming for some rest. All in all, you are not much better than a zombie on the Sunday. I usually watch the game on video but even then I don't really take it all in. It is a relief to get to work on Monday.

That week there was just the minor irritant of having to play a league match against Bath at the Recreation Ground. They had never lost there in the league. Somewhat to my surprise we came away with a win nicked from under their noses in the very last minute. I had barely thought about the game and as a result went in quite relaxed. Perhaps there is a lesson to be learned there.

The days were rushing by. The clock was ticking and there was little time to draw breath and think about it all. Probably just as well really. Nerves can cripple you. But even if we had had a month on a sandy beach to lie around fretting and worrying, we would never have got quite as uptight as we did before the Welsh match. France was going to be a day to remember.

There was also no time to dwell on the prospects because we actually had a lot to do as a team before the match. Certainly as a threequarter line we had a lot to work on. That Sunday morning at Twickenham we worked with Mike Slemen on alignment, depth and angle of running. We had been too cramped against Ireland, a sure sign that we had been anxious.

We had also kicked too much and not very well against Ireland. With the wind at your back there is always a temptation to hoist it and let the elements do the work. In fact looking at the video, the correct decision might have been to move it. Again, the old failing of getting a bit too fraught had blocked the mind to this. Relax. Relax. That was the key to success. Richard Hill thought exactly the same too. He had over-hit his kicks in Dublin, the result of too much adrenalin and not enough calculation. Relax. Relax. And it would all come good.

Monday and Tuesday – did they actually exist that week? They flew by. Work to do, press to satisfy, long-lost friends to try and find tickets for, an eight-month-old daughter to talk to at three in the morning. What a giddy mix. I was glad when Wednesday evening arrived. I left work early and headed for the team hotel in Richmond.

It has taken me five years to work out that if I drive to Richmond then I have to get a taxi back there on Sunday morning after the dinner at the Hilton to pick up my car. I took the tube and Will was due to meet me at the station. I was early so caught a cab to the hotel. There was not yet any buzz about the place but it would come I was sure.

By the time that game came round, I was carrying a whole suitcase of emotions round with me. Was I nervous or relaxed? Was I enjoying it all or was I scared stiff? Confident, terrified, calm, uptight, joky, bad-tempered? I just didn't know. I had a fixed grin when talking to some people and a solemn grimace with others. It was all wonderful; it was all horrible. Why am I doing this, I often ask myself on the Saturday morning of a big match? I could be in the pub, or on the golf course. Obviously, I need to do it and obviously I do enjoy it, but you would never think so in the hours leading up to a game. The best man at my wedding 18 months ago, Andy Davies, came to the hotel on Friday to pick up a ticket. He told me later that he could barely get a word of sense out of me.

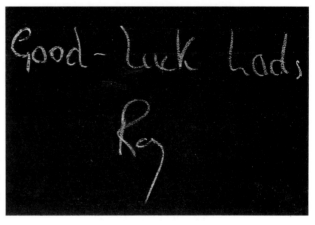

A message from the coach, Roger Uttley, in the dressing room before the final hurdle.

I doubt many other sportsmen go through such an intense period. Only in the World Cup do footballers come close to playing so many big games in such a short space of time. I suppose this year we were guilty of creating a lot of our own pressure. We badly wanted to win: indeed needed to win. As a result the emotional strain did at times almost become over-bearing. Some of the guys have said that they don't want to take too much more of it. Much as it drains you however, it also gives you a great buzz. The two are inseparable. It is a great test of your skill and character and only the best can cope with it. I have also thought about possible retirement and decided that I could not bear to see someone else in the white shirt while I was still fit enough compete for the position. I am only 28. Physically I am good for another few years yet. If someone else comes along who is better then me, then fair enough. Until then, whatever the emotional turmoil, I want as much of it as I can get. The low periods only make savouring the high moments that much sweeter.

There was a very different feel about the build-up to the Grand Slam match this year. Last time we were flying high, full of ourselves. We had been slick in training and ruthless on the pitch. This time we were having to work much harder at our game.

As a result we were far more prosaic and workmanlike in training. Our feet were firmly on the ground. And it was no bad thing.

There were however some lighter moments, such as the sweepstake on how long Paul Ackford would last before being thumped by the hard man, Tachdjian, whom France had brought in to their team. We talked a lot in those two days before the match about how we would take the game to them; about how our big back-row would take on the French and see how they liked being run at; about how we would try to unsettle Berbizier; about how we would rain kicks down on Blanco; about how alert we would be to French counter-attacks (so much for that one!); and about how hard we would be. The last factor was not just a simple cliché about toughing it out. There are hard men and there are hard men. In my book the real hard men are those that you hear little from, guys like Mike Teague, Jeff Probyn and Dean Richards, who just get on with what needs to be done. There was most definitely a tougher core to this team: it had more steel than the one which went down to Scotland last year. It would most certainly never yield until that final whistle sounded.

On Thursday afternoon we found a groundsman who would let us on to the pitch without having a nervous breakdown. The two full-backs, Simon and Jon Webb, plus myself and Richard Hill went through the whole repertoire of kicks. It went very well on the day, but it was because we gone through each and every kick so often beforehand. Blanco was bombarded a hundred times that Thursday afternoon. It was terrific to watch Simon Hodgkinson go through his routines. It was also terrific to watch him go through his routines in a match. For the simple reason, that it meant that I was not doing the goal-kicking. I never really relished the prospect. I kick for Wasps and have had a fair degree of success in internationals as well. However, it seems that my game has benefited now that Simon has taken over the responsibility. If the kicks are going over, then there's no real problem. But miss a couple, and no matter how tunnel-visioned you are, it does prey on your mind. Your outer game begins to suffer, which in turn means that the next kick you take is under even more pressure. So the spiral descends. Some fly-halves, such as Michael Lynagh and Grant Fox, cope brilliantly with it. I am sure I could do a fair job as well. Even so, for all the various reasons, I felt a lot happier seeing 'Hodgie' line up the kicks this season. He didn't do too badly, did he?

As a game gets closer, so we switch from being critical and negative about our last performance to being positive about what is to come, concentrating on our own strengths and on the weaknesses of our opponents. Geoff Cooke and Roger Uttley fade into the background: the players take over. We have to work it all out on the day:

we might as well work it out in training. That is how it evolved on Friday's session. The machine needed no more than a bit of oil here, a bit of fine tuning there. The real graft had been done long before. The way we eventually played against France had little to do with what we did that week. The victory was an accumulation of everything that had happened in the past few years: victory over Australia 1988; defeat against Wales and Scotland at the end of the last two seasons; running rugby against Ireland, Wales and France in 1990. It all pointed our way. Now, if only the game itself would get under way.

Time was the enemy. The perfect solution lay just five minutes down the road. 'Godfather III' was showing and about half the squad trooped down for the 4 o'clock showing. All very sensible. Except that no-one checked how long the film was. About three and a quarter hours to be precise, which meant that we were about half an hour late for the Friday team meeting. There was Will, the most important game of the season, all ready with the speech of a lifetime and only half a dozen guys to deliver it to. He was not best pleased.

It could have scuppered many a side. I am sure he just wanted to rip right into us but he chose not to. He handled it well. It was not the most heinous offence in the world, but it could have upset lesser men. As it was it just added an edge to proceedings which was probably what was needed anyway. Will went round the whole team asking them what it all meant for them, what they were going to work on, what they were going to contribute. It was the first time he had ever gone through the whole team. It worked. We all chipped in and by the end we knew that each part was going to function smoothly.

Sleep has never been a problem for me. Head on the pillow and away I go, dreaming of that elusive first-ever try for England, or of the Grand Slam-winning drop-goal for England in the dying moments with half of France hanging round my ankles. No problem for an Englishman: take that, you Froggie fiend, and the ball sails between the posts. Ah well, we can but dream. Some of the boys actually take sleeping pills to knock them out. Perhaps it is the self-imposed alcohol ban 48 hours prior to a match which leaves them a bit twitchy. Certainly the adrenalin charge takes some getting used to. In a normal working week I am in bed by 11 o'clock at the latest. Yet come England duty and I am frantically zapping through the TV control at midnight to see what else might be on.

The big day dawned. Hadn't we kicked off yet? I had already played the game over a hundred times in my mind and still there was over six hours to go. The weather looked good but we had been warned that it would deteriorate. How right they were.

As against Ireland however, it made no difference what the conditions were like. This side could cope with anything. If anything, the French would have spent the morning thumbing despondently through the dictionary trying to work out what 'cats and dogs by mid-afternoon' actually meant.

The hotel became progressively quieter that morning. There was a certain nervous hubbub at breakfast – cereal and poached eggs for me, fried delight for many of the forwards – which soon died down as the spectre of the match began to close in on us.

There was plenty to occupy us however. There were various meetings and we had to get packed so that our stuff could be moved over to the London Hilton where the post-match banquet was to be held. In between times we wandered aimlessly around the hotel exchanging banal pleasantries. 'All right, Will?' 'Actually, no, I think I've just broken my leg coming downstairs. Do you think you could tell Geoff Cooke for me?'

Ask a silly question. There were a few telegrams to open which is always a treat. Why do people think you might not appreciate them just because you have won a few caps. Good luck messages are always welcome. Ian Beer, headmaster as Harrow, Peter Yarranton from Wasps and one of the 'finds' of this season, my club-mate at Wasps, Damien Hopley, had all put pen to paper. The weirdest thing was watching the start of Grandstand just after midday. There was Twickenham, there was Des Lynam, there were all the actions shots and hype about England: but where were we? A few miles away slumped in the TV lounge wishing it were all over.

To the coach and off to the ground. Again, it was quiet, save for Tina Turner belting out on the stereo and Dewi Morris dishing out goodies from the huge bag of sweets he normally keeps for the boys on the bench. Most of us were wrapped up in our thoughts. The final check list: kicks to touch; kicks from hand; tackles; catches; alignment; moves. They were all in order. We had a police escort so we cut through the traffic with ease. It seemed busier than usual. Normally the A316 to Twickenham is fairly clear at this time as are the pavements. Usually the crowd are intent on their warm-up for the game in the local pubs. Not today. Whether it was because they wanted to get there early to soak up atmosphere or whether they were cutting down on the booze to ensure that they could remember the day itself, I don't know. But there they were, in their raucous thousands.

Twickenham has become a great place to play at. It always was an honour to play there, but these days it has a real buzz about in on match days. In the bad old times, as long as the claret was the right temperature in the car park beforehand, and

TOP *Ackford makes a superb two-handed catch.*
ABOVE *England's early pressure is rewarded with a penalty by the posts.*

as long as the chaps gave it a good shot, then it did not really matter who won or lost. Now the crowd are in there fighting every last inch of the way with you. Victory is important to them.

In this respect Twickenham has become as intimidating a place for visiting teams as Cardiff used to be. It is not just the 15 guys on the field they are competing against: there are 55,000 more all around the ground willing them to defeat. England have only lost twice there in the last seven seasons. I am not quite sure why a crowd should make such a difference, but they do. Not so much at the start of a game but in the last quarter. No matter how hard you have trained, no matter how hardened your mind is, your body will eventually begin to sag. It is then that you need a shot of crowd-induced adrenalin to get you riding back up there through the land where pain does not exist. Only the All Blacks seem to have come to terms with playing away from home which is probably not surprising given that that is where most of their international rugby is played: but that is on tour when preparation is so much better.

That afternoon Twickenham was every bit as charged emotionally as Murrayfield had been the year before. It was like a zoo arriving at the ground at about 1:15, thousands of faces pressed up to our coach and then having to run the gauntlet to the changing-rooms. No time to stop, not even for my wife Sara whom I had spotted from the bus.

The changing room was a sanctuary of sorts, although that too filled up with various officials and the like popping in to offer their best wishes. I am afraid I now to dispel a long-held myth. No, the forwards don't go round head-butting each other or biting each other or even slapping faces. They are quiet and in control, reining back their energy rather than trying to boost it up. They have no need for false stimulation: it is all there inside.

We went out for the team photograph about 40 minutes before kick-off. There was more noise than normal. The crowd were already in place and you could sense that something special was about to happen. I had already walked the four corners of the pitch to test out the wind. As usual, it was a south-westerly, coming in from that direction and sweeping round the stands. Now that the new North stand is in place however, the wind can escape. With the old stand, up tight to the pitch, the wind would bounce back out again and follow the West stand down the ground, running in the opposite direction to the breeze on the other side: the so-called Twickenham swirl. It took some getting used to.

There was little else to say or do. Smurf, physiotherapist Kevin Murphy,

Rob Andrew on the attack, shepherded by Winterbottom, Teague and Ackford.

checks he has got spare contact lenses for Paul Ackford and myself, a final stretch, a bit of jogging to work up a sweat, a final word from Will, 'Let's not go through what we did last year, eh?' and on to the pitch.

And so to the game, and to the final whistle. It went that quickly and it went that well. Even after Saint-André scored 'that try' I was not worried. We were playing as well as we had done all season and his try only had the scores at 6-3. No problem. They could only score if they had the ball and there were eight men in white shirts making very sure that they would see very little of the ball that afternoon. Matches are won and lost up front. This Grand Slam was built around our forwards. They were magnificent. The only tremble of anxiety came with Mesnel's late try. We were guilty of clock-watching, particularly in the threequarters. Should I kick long or short at the re-start? The brain would not work. I went long; I have no idea why.

The whistle and it was all over. What scenes. The relief, the fatigue, the numbness, the pain, the confusion, the crowd, the crowd, all around, and such joy, such sweet joy. In the dressing-room, more happy chaos. What had happened didn't really sink in . I was too shattered. It didn't even hit home that night as we caroused our way through many celebrations. It will though. You do not forget days like that in a hurry.

Didier Camberabero scores to keep France in touch.

I thought that I might get emotional in the build-up to the French game, but I didn't. No nerves, no apprehension, no excitement, no fear. It was all very business-like which is just the sort of approach we needed to take. Let the French get emotional: that was their style. Let the English be reserved and calm: that was our style. It was the great conflict of opposites and one that I was sure we would win.

Tuning my mind into the victory wavelength was not that easy after Leicester travelled down to Bristol the Saturday before for a league match and lost. We were dreadful. No-one wanted to know. Our showing was a poor reflection on the club and had not left me in the best of moods as Rory drove us up to London. I was even more disgruntled to find that of the forwards all bar Wade had had an afternoon off. That meant they would be raring to go for Sunday training while muggins here creaked and groaned his way around. Wade had played for Preston Grasshoppers against Lichfield. I just don't know how he does it, playing at what is obviously a markedly lower standard of rugby yet getting himself back up there for the internationals. He does it his way and I do it mine, I suppose. I need hard rugby to keep me sharp: he is the opposite. It takes all sorts.

My worst fears were confirmed that Sunday morning. It was a hard session and the other boys revelled in it. The 'B' team also had a game against France to prepare for and so we did a lot of contact work using them as opposition. The line-outs were well contested which is always a good thing to be able to get used to, particularly against the French.

I played a season for Roanne in France just after I had left school. French club rugby is without doubt the dirtiest in the world. They even practise how to take a man out of the game. On the one hand, they play the game like no other side can, full of grace and beauty: on the other, they will kick the living daylights out of you if they get near you. A strange mix. We were ready for it. Even at international level where it is difficult to get away with anything, the French would try it on. There was no doubt about it, particularly in the scrum with fists and fingers coming through all afternoon long. Quite how they had the nerve to say before this year's game that England had been ungentlemanly in previous years is beyond me. Ask Gareth Chilcott about 1989 ago and he will show you a few marks around his eyes which he certainly did not get from putting on his make-up that morning.

The prospect of a hard match did not worry us in the slightest. We had a lot of respect for Les Peard and knew that if anything started he would sort it out pretty quickly. We also knew that they were likely to be more afraid of us then we of them. As it turned out, despite bringing in two supposed 'hit-men' in Benazzi and Tachdjian they were nowhere near as bad as they had been in the past. Perhaps we just did not allow them to be.

I was surprised they could afford to leave out a number 8 of the calibre of Cécillon. He is a good accomplished player as was shown when he came on to replace Tachdjian during the game. Tachdjian should have been in Los Angles for the Oscars a couple of weeks later such was his performance at feigning injury.

We looked at how to combat Roumat in the line-out. He had won a lot of ball that season, a lot of it with the assistance of those around him. Fair enough, if you can get away with it. We had little intention of letting him get away with it and planned to drive hard and low at the middle of the line. Roumat also had a tendency to stand out and come back into the line which meant that we might be able to nudge him out of the game.

Blanco was an obvious threat. From a forwards' point of view we noted that he often attacked down the blind-side. Much to the dismay of the front five, but certainly not to their surprise, I proposed that I should come off early from the scrum to counter this move. 'What's different from normal?' they yelled. The fact that after all these years France had actually selected specialist open and blind-side flankers affected our thinking. Cabannes would be out there competing for the loose ball with Winters which of course meant that our support had to be quicker. More significantly it meant that we had to keep their back-row on the move, making them work on the retreat. We planned to drive hard at the scrums well as in the loose. Cabannes had also won a lot of line-outs that season thanks to the long throw over the top. We had to work out a defence for that.

The final factor which came out in the pre-match planning was our need to chase kicks more vigorously. Rob and Richard were planning to use the kick to exert pressure: the back-row and the centres were the means by which we applied this pressure. We had been slack at this in the past but could not afford to be against the type of runners that France had.

TOP *'We're 40 minutes from glory - let's not blow it this time.'*
ABOVE **Mike Teague and Dean Richards prepare to spoil Serge Blanco's farewell Championship appearance.**

It was in this planning stage that the game was won. Virtually everything we had targeted came off. It makes all the effort worthwhile if, come the game, you can see the expected patterns unfolding before you. It gives your confidence a huge boost, knowing that if all continues to go well, that you will win.

I am not a particularly late bird and was in bed by about 11 p.m. that Friday evening, having given Jerry Guscott a good seeing-to on the cribbage table. The early night did me no good whatsoever. I was awake by 5 a.m. and had to kill two hours lying there while Brian Moore snored on. The morning stretched away before me. There was simply nothing else left to do except get out their on the pitch and give the French a good hiding.

There was far more commotion around Twickenham than normal, everyone in the car park giving it their best shot. I tried to block out all feelings, all negative thoughts. All I wanted was for the whistle to blow. I was desperate to get stuck into the action. Once that happened any nerves there were would disappear.

I am a slow changer and I am certainly not a head-banger. Read the programme, disappear to the smallest room in the stadium for some peace and then a gentle build-up to kick-off. There was very little noise where I was, just a few of the

The sight all opponents fear - Simon Hodgkinson lining up a goal kick.

The final whistle.

The Barnard Castle boys, Rob Andrew and Rory Underwood, celebrate the Grand Slam.

forwards stretching off in the shower area. There was nothing much to say, although I almost blew it when I went up to Ackers and said: 'Let's have a good day then, sir.' He told me later that I had almost knocked him out of his stride. There he was, getting geared up to die for his country and I burst the bubble by addressing him as 'sir'.

Twickenham was superb that afternoon. To hear the national anthem belted out and the noise later when we edged in front was brilliant. I felt like joining in with the singing in the stands at one stage but thought better of it. It gave us a lift, there is no doubt about it. I am also sure that it intimidated the French. Certainly when you looked across at them at the first line-out you could see that they weren't quite into it. Hard yes; but not quite prepared to put their neck right down there on the chopping block. Unlike the Irish they were not prepared to go the extra mile. We kept them at work so perhaps that is why they were never able to come back at us. All in all their forwards were fairly quiet, even on the niggle front.

It was our best performance of the season up front. We had a lot of control and worked up a head of steam in the loose. We had not really managed to get much drive in the mauls all year. Here we did, with good protection of the ball as well. Winters knocked down the first man every time, which meant that we always had a target to drive onto. Mike Teague got through a huge amount of work and was instrumental in leading our charges. In the scrummage I was most impressed by Jason Leonard. He was up against one of the wiliest campaigners around in Pascal Ondarts but there was not a murmur from Jason. He just got on with the game.

There was a strong current of confidence running through the side which would have been impossible to stem. Certainly Saint-André's try caused little more than a ripple in the ranks. The game was ours and no matter where they ran from, we knew that we would soon be back at them. So it proved.

The final whistle and what pandemonium. I hurtled for the tunnel alongside Les Peard. Jerry Guscott went down amidst all the mayhem so the two of us had to drag him clear. I must say that in retrospect I quite envied the lads still out there being carried shoulder high. It looked good fun. There was quite some celebrating in the dressing room, although I was a bit miffed at all the champagne being wasted by being sprayed around. It was a great night, one of the best I can remember after an international. It wasn't just the victory and the Grand Slam. There was a very real feeling of friendship amongst the squad, the boys on the bench having contributed a huge amount, and it was good to savour the achievement with them all. The wives and girlfriends had also become very much part of the scene which made for a terrific night out.

There is no doubt in my mind as to the best moment of the day however, even of the whole season. As the initial celebration started in the dressing room I slipped away on my own to the bath. I just lay there, letting it all sink it. It felt good; so very good.

A champagne end to a great season.

Prayer answered, mission accomplished.

The Squad

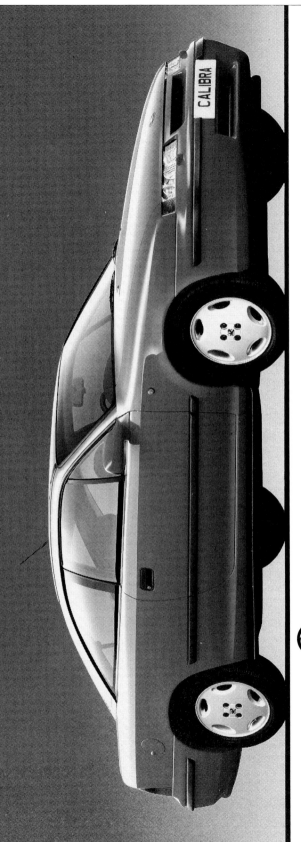

SWEET CHARIOT.

VAUXHALL Once driven, forever smitten.

THE TEAM

WILL CARLING (Harlequins)
Born: 12.12.65, Bradford-on-Avon, Wiltshire
Age: 25
Height 5'11"
Weight: 13st 12lbs
Position: Centre
Caps: 24
Points: 12 (3T)
Internationals: 1988 F,W,S,I(1,2),A(2) Fj,A
1989 S,I,F,W,Fj 1990 I,F,W,S,Arg (1,2),Arg
1991 W,S,I,F

Educated at Sedbergh and Durham University, Will Carling resigned his commission in the Army in 1988 and now runs his own marketing company, Inspirational Horizons. Much to his own surprise he was appointed captain against Australia in 1988 since which time he has become his country's most successful skipper, having led England to victory in 13 of his 17 matches in charge. He missed the Lions tour to Australia in 1989 because of a recurring shin problem, an injury which opened the door for his partner in the centre, Jeremy Guscott.
Comment:(RA) *Will has borne the responsibility of being captain superbly. He does an awful lot of work off the field with the the players which goes unnoticed. As a centre he has great pace and power, qualities which are the ideal foil to Jerry Guscott. It's difficult to find weaknesses in his game and if there were any glaring ones you could be sure that he would work on them immediately. He is so committed.*

SIMON HODGKINSON (Nottingham)
Born: 15.12.62, Bristol
Age: 28
Height: 5'10"
Weight: 12st 5lbs
Position: Full-back
Caps: 13
Points: 186 (1T, 31C, 40PG)
Internationals: 1989 Ro,Fj 1990 I,F,W,S,Arg (1,2),
Arg 1991 W,S,I,F

Educated at Stamford School and Trent Polytechnic, Simon Hodgkinson has a BA in Business Studies. He taught Economics at Trent College before moving into commerce with HFS, a finance company in Macclesfield. He has re-written the record books since he first came into the England side two years ago. His 60 points is a new Five Nations record, eclipsing the 44 points England total of Dusty Hare and the Championship mark of 54 points set by Lescarboura. Against Argentina in November he amassed a national record 23 points; against Wales he kicked a world record seven penalties; his total of 18 penalties is a record for a Championship season. He has also played fly-half for Nottingham, the club he joined in 1981.
Comment(RA): *His goal-kicking speaks for itself. Certainly it has settled the side on so many occasions. What is ignored about Simon is the calming influence he exerts on the team. He himself is very collected whilst in defence he rarely makes errors, a failing which we had been prone to on occasions in the past. He may not be the biggest, strongest or fastest but when he comes into the line he invariably makes the right decision. He also has good hands as was shown when linking for Nigel Heslop's try against Scotland and Rory Underwood's in Dublin. A fine all-round footballer.*

NIGEL HESLOP (Orrell)
Born: 4.12.63, Hartlepool
Age: 27
Height: 5'10"
Weight: 12st 7lbs
Position: Wing
Caps: 7
Points: 8 (2T)
Internationals: 1990 Arg(1,2),Arg 1991 W,S,I,F

Educated at Rainford High School, St Helens, Nigel Heslop is a police officer stationed at Newton-le-Willows, Lancashire. He began playing rugby when 14 and quickly won representative honours for Lancashire and then England Colts. He partnered Rory Underwood in a colts international against France in 1981 but that was the last he saw of him as an England team-mate until the 1990-91 season. Nigel played for Liverpool and Waterloo before moving to Orrell.
Comment(RA): *It's a measure of Nigel's contribution to our success that no-one can say that he looked out of place in any game. He took his try well against Scotland and often showed himself to be difficult to handle in attack. He put in some tremendous clearing kicks from defence and was a great target for the forwards to hit in attack.*

JEREMY GUSCOTT (Bath)
Born: 7.7.65, Bath
Age: 25
Height: 6'1"
Weight: 13st 5lbs
Position: Centre
Caps: 11
Points: 36 (9T)
Internationals: 1989 Ro,Fj 1990 I,F,W,S,Arg
1991 W,S,I,F
British Lions 1989 A (2,3)

Educated at Ralph Allen School, Bath, Jeremy Guscott is a public relations officer for British Gas having formerly been a bricklayer and occasional male model. Jeremy sprung to prominence at the end of the 1989 season when an injury to Will Carling allowed him to win his first cap against Romania. He took full advantage, scoring a hat-trick of tries to crown a performance which won him a late call to the Lions party for Australia. He made the side for the last two Tests, scoring a crucial try in the Sydney game. He has played all his rugby at Bath starting with the under-7s.
Comment(RA): *Jerry is an outstanding player which means that it was something of a pity we did not see more of his talent this season. His great asset is his change of pace, the startling ability to glide past players from a standing start. What are often overlooked are his defensive qualities, much in evidence against France. He has the pace to get out wide and in the final game was instrumental in putting Blanco under so much pressure that he had a restricted game. He has that rare touch of class in everything he does.*

RORY UNDERWOOD (Leicester and RAF)
Born: 19.6.63, Middlesborough
Age: 27
Height: 5' 9"
Weight 13st 7lbs
Position: Wing
Caps: 43
Points: 108 (27T)
Internationals: 1984 I,F,W,A 1985 Ro,F,S,I,W 1986 W,I,F 1987 I,F,W,S (W.Cup) A,J,W 1988 F,W,S,I(1,2), A(1,2),Fj,A 1989 S,I,F,W,Ro,Fj 1990 I,F,W,S,Arg 1991 W,S,I,F
British Lions 1989 A (1,2,3)

Educated at Barnard Castle School, Durham, Rory

Underwood joined the RAF shortly after leaving school. He spent many years in an England shirt and barely saw the ball. It is only during the Geoff Cooke regime that Rory's undoubted talent has blossomed. His try against France extended his England record to 27. That match also saw Underwood equal Tony Neary's record total of 43 appearances for England. Rory also jointly holds the England record of 5 tries in an international, achieved against Fiji in 1989.
Comment: (RA) *Rory is a world-class finisher and always has been. If anything he has even improved on those skills. Some of his tries in the last two or three seasons would not have been scored by any other wing in the world. What he has added to his game is a willingness to get more involved. He used to drift out of the action. He has rectified that and also improved his all-round defence.*

ROB ANDREW (Wasps)
Born: 18.2.63, Richmond, Yorkshire
Age: 28
Height: 5' 9"
Weight: 12st 3lbs
Position: Fly-half
Caps: 36
Points: 132 (9C,28P,10DG)
Internationals: 1985 Ro,F,S,I,W 1986 W,S,I,F 1987 I,F,W, (W.Cup) J(R),Am 1988 S,I(1,2) A(1,2), Fj,A 1989 S,I,F,W,Ro,Fj 1990 I,F,W,S,Arg 1991 W,S,I,F
British Lions 1989 A (2,3)

Educated at Barnard Castle School, Durham, where he was a contemporary of Rory Underwood, Rob Andrew went on to Cambridge University and from there into business where he is a chartered surveyor with Debenham, Tewson and Chinnocks. Rob is England's most capped fly-half, an accolade which at one point in his career looked a rather distant prospect. However, having been summoned as a replacement for the Lions tour in 1989, his play and confidence have matured greatly, to the extent that he was one of the most influential figures in the 1991 Grand Slam side. He is a double blue, having captained Cambridge at cricket.
Comment(DR): *He has been the most improved fly-half in the world these last few years. He exerts great control on a game and rarely lets the forwards down by wasting possession. His awareness of the options available and his decision-making are first-class.*

RICHARD HILL (Bath)
Born: 4.5.61, Birmingham
Age: 29
Height: 5' 7"
Weight: 12st 6lb
Position: Scrum-half
Caps: 21
Points: 8 (2T)
Internationals: 1984 SA (1,2) 1985 I(R),NZ(2R)
1986 F(R) 1987 I,F,W (W.Cup) Am. 1989 Fj
1990 I,F,W,S Arg(1,2), Arg 1991 W,S,I,F

Educated at Bishop Wordsworth's School, Salisbury and Exeter University, Richard Hill's career has had two distinct phases. He has played in all England's last 12 internationals, having been only an occasional performer in his early years, three of his caps having been won from the bench. Then, just when it seemed he had achieved a certain stability, he was one of four players disciplined by the RFU following the ill-tempered game against Wales in 1987. Richard reappraised his entire approach and has not looked back since. He works for a financial consultancy, Noble Lowndes, in Bristol.

Comment (RA): *Richard has a history a bit very like my own. If anything he has been more out in the wilderness than me. For him to have come back after being dumped as England captain speaks volumes for his character. He learned his lesson all round. His game is now more varied, choosing shrewdly between working with the back-row and spinning it wide. If, for example, Robert Jones or Nigel Melville have a more natural pass, then you would not notice the difference in efficiency these days because Richrd has worked so hard to make his polished. A world-class performer.*

JASON LEONARD (Harlequins)
Born: 14.8.68, Barking
Age: 22
Height: 5'10"
Weight: 16st 8lb
Position: Loose-head prop
Caps: 7
Internationals: 1990 Arg(1,2), Arg 1991 W,S,I,F

Educated at Warren Comprehensive, Jason Leonard is the youngest member of the team, having come into the sqaud for the summer tour to Argentina in 1990 and making his début in the first Test. He came through the colts section of his club, Barking, before moving to Saracens. He joined Harlequins after the Argentina tour in order to further his experience by playing alongside seasoned internationals. He is a self-employed carpenter.

Comment (DR): *Young, talented and taken great strides this season. He is already a good player and is destined for a great future, especially as he is very eager to learn. I have been most impressed by his scrummaging which has come on by leaps and bounds.*

BRIAN MOORE (Harlequins)
Born: 11.1.62, Birmingham
Age: 29
Height: 5' 9"
Weight: 14st 5lb
Position: Hooker
Caps: 29
Points: 4 (1T)
Internationals: 1987 S, (W.Cup) A,J,W
1988 F,W,S,I(1,2) A(1,2), Fj,A 1989 S,I,F,W.Ro,Fj
1990 I,F,W,S Arg (1,2) 1991 W,S,I,F
British Lions 1989 A (1,2,3)

Educated at Crossley & Porter HS, Halifax, Brian Moore obtained a law degree at Nottingham Univeristy from where he passed into local practice. Last summer he moved to London to take up a position as a corporate financier and joined Harlequins. He has established himself as the leading hooker in the British Isles having played in all three Tests for the Lions in 1989. He joined Nottingham in 1981 and later became captain. He played for England students in 1982 and toured Italy, Romania and Spain with England U-23s. Since winning his first cap against Scotland in 1987 he has missed only two matches.

Comment(DR): *I wouldn't enjoy playing against Brian, that's for sure, if only for the reason that he talks too much. He is an awkward customer and won't let an opponent rest at all during a match. A terrific competitor.*

JEFF PROBYN (Wasps)
Born: 27.4.56, London
Age: 35
Height: 5'10"
Weight: 15st 10lb
Position: Tight-head prop
Caps: 22
Points: 8 (2T)
Internationals: 1988 F,W,S,I(1,2), A(1,2), A
1989 S,I,Ro(R) 1990 I,F,W,S, Arg(1,2), Arg
1991 W,S,I,F

Educated at the London Nautical School, Jeffrey Probyn is a company director in his own reproduction furniture business. He won his first cap relatively late in life against France in 1988. He has played on either side of the scrummage in a rugby career which has taken him from Old Albanians to Ilford Wanderers, Streatham-Croydon, Richmond, and then Wasps.

Comment(DR): *The best tight head in the world in my book. He has great strength, unrivalled technique and will not cede an inch to anyone. Yet he is still one of the game's gentlemen.*

PAUL ACKFORD (Harlequins)
Born: 26.2.58, Hanover, West Germany
Age: 33
Height: 6' 6"
Weight: 17st 7lbs
Position: Lock
Caps: 16
Points: 4 (1T)
Internationals: 1988 A 1989 S,I,F,W,Ro, Fj 1990
I,F,W,S,Arg 1991 W,S,I,F
British Lions: 1989 A (1,2,3)

Educated at Plymouth College, Devon before going on to Kent and Cambridge Universities. He was an English teacher at Dulwich College before joining the police force where he has quickly risen to the rank of inspector and is currently based at Clapham. He had to wait until he was 30 before winning his first cap despite having played for England 'B' when he was only 21. He has played for Plymouth Albion, Rosslyn Park and Met Police. His move to Harlequins four years ago triggered a change in his fortunes.

Comment(DR): *'The Boss'. He has mastered the art of number two jumping at which he has no equal in the world. He has also proved himself to be a superb athlete, getting round the field with amazing speed. Will stand his ground, until he receives a sideways punch.*

WADE DOOLEY (Preston Grasshoppers)
Born: 2.10.57, Warrington
Age: 33
Height: 6' 8"
Weight: 17st 10lb
Position: Lock
Caps: 41
Points: 8 (2T)
Internationals: 1985 Ro,F,S,I,W,NZ(R,2)
1986 W,S,I,F 1987 F,W (W.Cup) A,AM,W
1988 F,W,S,I(1,2), A(1,2),Fj,A 1989 S,I,F,W,Ro,Fj
1990 I,F,W,S,Arg(1,2),Arg 1991 W,S,I,F
British Lions 1989 A (2,3)

Educated at Beaumont Secondary School, Warrington, Wade Dooley joined the police force on leaving school. He is currently a community beat officer in Blackpool. He played rugby league at school and might have been to content to play only junior club rugby if he had not come to the attention of former England coach, Dick Greenwood. His recommendation saw Dooley rise to prominence. Dooley has more than justified Greenwood's faith in him having passed Bill Beaumont's record of most caps for an England second row during the summer tour to Argentina. He has played in the last 28 games in succession for England.

Comment(DR): *'The Tower'. The man is impossible to fault. He is a real power in the scrum, climbs to great heights in the line-out and gets round the field like a back-row. Unflappable off the field.*

MIKE TEAGUE (Gloucester)
Born: 8.10.59, Gloucester
Age: 31
Height: 6' 3"
Weight: 16st 6lb
Position: Flanker
Caps: 15
Points: 16 (4T)
Internationals: 1985 F(R),NZ(1,2) 1989 S,I,F,W,Ro
1990 F,W,S 1991 W,S,I,F
British Lions 1989 A (2,3)

Educated at Churchdown School, Gloucester, Mike Teague has spent most of his life in his home town of Gloucester where we works in the family building business. Mike Teague was a 'B' international at the age of 22 and went on to tour South Africa with England in 1984. He went to New Zealand in 1985 where a heavy defeat convinced him that his England days were numbered. He almost gave up rugby but came back to achieve one of the highest individual accolades in the game, being voted Player of the Series in the 1989 British Lions tour to Australia.
Comment(DR): *A real grafter who gets through a tremendous amount of work in a game. He has immense upper body strength as well as stamina round the field. What is not appreciated is how talented a ball player he is.*

DEAN RICHARDS (Leicester)
Born: 11.7.63, Nuneaton
Age: 27
Height: 6' 3"
Weight: 17st 3lb
Position: Number 8
Caps: 25
Points: 24 (6T)
Internationals: 1986 I,F 1987 S (W.Cup) A,J,AM,W
1988 F,W,S,I,A (1,2),Fj,A 1989 S,I,F,W,Ro
1990 Arg 1991 W,S,I,F
British Lions A (1,2,3)

Educated at John Cleveland College, Hinckley, Dean Richards spent a year in France before joining the police force. He switched to number 8 after winning a schools cap in the second-row. He scored two tries on his début for England against Ireland and might have had a hat-trick but for a collapsed Irish scrummage. His career has been thwarted by injury, causing him to miss much of the 1987 season as well as the entire programme in 1990.
Comment(RA): *A one-off. Dean is a unique man and a unique talent. He looks ungainly, with socks rolled down and shirt hanging out, yet is the shrewdest player I've ever come across on a rugby field. He has made a big difference being back in the team this year. Perhaps we haven't played the ball as wide because he's there. And why bother? You know that if Dean has the ball in his hands there is no-one in the world who is going to get it off him. He enjoys huge respect from everyone, including the opposition. He is unorthodox in all that he does. Yet however he manages to do it, he does it. He has the best hands in the game and there is no doubt that of all the fine players in our side that he is very genuinely a world-class performer. He has no equal.*

PETER WINTERBOTTOM (Harlequins)
Born: 31.5.60, Leeds
Age: 30
Height: 6'
Weight: 14st 12lb
Position: Flanker
Caps: 42
Points: 8 (2T)
Internationals: 1982 A,S,I,F,W 1983 F,W,S,I,NZ
1984 S,F,W,SA(1,2) 1986 W,S,I,F 1987 I,F,W
(W.Cup) A,J,Am,W 1988 F,W,S 1989 Ro,Fj
1990 I,F,W,S, Arg (1,2),Arg 1991 W,S,I,F
British Lions 1983 NZ (1,2,3,4)

Educated at Rossall School, Peter Winterbottom is one of the world's most travelled rugby players. He has spent many summers playing club rugby in New Zealand and South Africa. Only in recent years has he adopted a more settled lifestyle after moving to London to take up a position as a Eurobond dealer in the City. He is the most senior member of the party although Rory Underwood has just beaten him to the joint English record for the most caps. He was captain of Headingley before moving to Harlequins.
Comment(DR): *He puts his head where others would fear even to stand. His ball handling has improved enormously now that he is playing more sevens. The best and hardest tackler in the game.*

THE REPLACEMENTS

J.M. WEBB (Bath)
S.J. HALLIDAY (Bath)
D.P. HOPLEY (Wasps)
C.D. MORRIS (Orrell)
P.A.G. RENDALL (Wasps)
C.J. OLVER (Northampton)
M.G. SKINNER (Harlequins)

THE MANAGEMENT

GEOFF COOKE (Manager)
Born: 11.6.41
Age: 49
Educated: Carlisle GS
Job: Chief Executive British Institute of Sports Coaches

Fly-half/centre for Bradford and Cumbria. Yorkshire coach. Divisional manager 1979-86. North team manager 1986-87. England manager October 1987-
Comment(RA): *Geoff has been almost single-handedly responsible for our success over the last three years. The players were always there. It's just that there was no system within which they could operate. Geoff has set that up and has also instilled a great sense of unity by pledging his faith in players. We are now all going in the same direction.*

ROGER UTTLEY (Coach)
Born: 11.9.49
Age: 41
Educated: Blackpool GS
Job: Schoolmaster, Harrow School

Lock, number 8 or flanker for Gosforth, Wasps and Northumberland. Won first cap in 1973, toured South Africa with Lions in 1974 and was a member of England's Grand Slam side in 1980.   London coach 1985-87. England coach December 1987-
Comment(RA): *Roger has won a lot of respect from the players for his honesty and straight-talking. His main work has been with the forwards who obviously benefited from his immense playing experience. Apart from that he has not imposed himself heavily on the players, leaving them to conduct operations as they see fit. The squad has responded well to this sense of independence.*

JOHN ELLIOTT (Selector)
Born: 10.6.43
Age: 47
Educated: High Pavement School
Job: Head of Market Development, East Midlands Electricity.

Hooker for Old Paviors, Leicester, Nottingham. England replacement 1976. Coach Notts, Lincs and Derby. Midlands selector 1981-86. England selector October 1987-
Comment(RA): *John is the back seat man who does all the unseen work. Without him things would not flow smoothly and he is obviously an important part of the team. He gets on very well with the players and is a great sounding-board at team meetings.*

World Cup
Prospects

T he Grand Slam triumph has been a tremendous shot in the arm for English rugby and if it means nothing else it guarantees that we will be taken very seriously by all our opponents in the World Cup in October. In the Five Nations Championship we have only lost two of our last 12 matches over a 3 year period and both of these defeats were away matches at Cardiff and Murrayfield.

We have proved this year that we are the best side in Europe and it has generally been acknowledged that we deserved to win all four matches and the Championship. This does not mean the World Cup is there for the taking but it does mean that if we can improve our overall performance by 10 or 15 per cent we have a very real chance of beating New Zealand in the opening match of the tournament and that would present us with a fantastic opportunity of reaching the final.

There is no doubt that the game against the All Blacks on October 3rd is of absolutely crucial importance. If we win that game the strong likelihood, assuming we beat Italy and the United States, is that we would meet Fiji in the quarter-final at Lille. This makes the reasonable assumption at this stage that France will beat Fiji in their pool match and that both these sides will be too good for Romania and Canada.

We would certainly be expected to beat Fiji and that would put us through to a semi-final match against Australia, Scotland or Ireland in Dublin. If we won that match then there is every chance we would meet New Zealand again in the final as they would be strongly fancied to win through in the other half of the draw.

On the other hand, if we lose our opening match to the All Blacks, our route to the final will be much more hazardous. We would have to play France in Paris in the quarter-final and if we won that we would then be at Murrayfield for our semi-final. That would almost certainly be against Scotland or Ireland because whichever side wins their pool 2 clash would play Wales at Murrayfield in the first quarter-final.

It seems then that our hopes of winning the World Cup depend largely on the outcome of our game against New Zealand in the first of the 32 matches in the competition. A couple of years ago the All Blacks would have been warm favourites for such a game but I firmly believe now that we deserve to be slight favourites.

After an incredible run of 23 Tests without defeat since 1986 when they lost to France in Nantes, they did not look quite so formidable and invincible last summer. First of all Scotland came desperately close to beating them in the second Test in Auckland when they led by 3 points and only lost to two late controversial penalties. Scotland also did well in the first Test and went unbeaten in the six provincial matches which was a great achievement. `Scotland were the Grand Slam champions last summer and did so well against the All Blacks that many people felt that if the two Tests had been played at Murrayfield and not in New Zealand then Scotland would have won at least one of them. We will enjoy home advantage when we play the All Blacks in the World Cup and that could well make a critical difference.

There was further evidence last summer that the All Blacks are not quite the force they were in the late 1980s. After winning the first two Tests against Australia in the Bledisloe Cup series, Australia won the third Test in Wellington by 21 points to 9. That proved, if proof were necessary, this current All Black side can be beaten. What Australia did last August, England can do this October. There is no pack in the world which our forwards need to fear but, having said that, I would suggest that, at the moment, the English and New Zealand packs are the best two in world rugby and our World Cup showdown promises to be an explosive encounter of massive passion and intensity.

It should be well worthwhile crossing a field of broken glass in bare feet just to watch the respective front-rows trying to gain supremacy in the scrums. Leonard, Moore and Probyn against McDowell, Fitzpatrick and Loe. Ian Jones and Gary Whetton are both top line-out men, but the English camp is adamant that we hold the advantage through Paul Ackford and Wade Dooley. Furthermore, our two locks are dynamic scrummagers and outstanding in the loose.

I would also argue that we have a major, clear-cut advantage at number 8 where not only has Dean Richards had a quite phenomenal season for England and proved himself the best player in his position in the world, but, for once, New Zealand are struggling to find a player to match their two stars of the 1980s, Murray Mexted and Wayne Shelford. Zinzan Brooke has played a few disappointing games since he took over and it is unlikely that the All Blacks will recall Wayne Shelford at this late stage of his career. In France in the autumn, Mike Brewer was given a chance but he does not look an out and out All Black number 8 and it is unquestionably a problem position for them at the moment.

At blind-side flanker Mike Teague will not yield an inch to Alan Whetton and the open-side contest will depend very much on whether Michael Jones has regained full fitness and recaptures completely the fantastic form he showed early on in his international career before being badly injured. What is so fascinating is that on paper

Winning Grand Slams is a serious business for England manager, Geoff Cooke - winning World Cups even more so.

it looks like stalemate and we will not know for certain who will win the forward battle, and with it almost certainly the match, until the game itself. All the hypothesising is great fun but fairly futile. The game will be an intriguing battle of contrasting styles. We will see the famous New Zealand rucking against the now perhaps equally famous England mauling.

It is very hard to predict who will take control. To make a riveting contest even more unpredictable, it is hard to say which back division can claim the greater strike power. I would definitely rate Richard Hill a better all-round scrum-half than Graeme Bachop and would give the edge at centre in attack to Will Carling and Jeremy Guscott. This is not to suggest that Craig Innes and Walter Little are not very good centres because they are, but on their day at their very best Will and Jeremy should be the best centre partnership in the World Cup.

On the wing the genius of Rory Underwood is more or less cancelled out by John Kirwan and I suppose the huge depth of international experience which Terry Wright has accrued over the years may give him some advantage on the other wing. The defection of full-back John Gallagher to Rugby League was a massive blow to New Zealand and his disappearance has left a huge void. Crowley is the current choice and he is a good footballer but he is certainly not another John Gallagher.

Even the one area in which the All Blacks have excelled for several seasons – goal-kicking – is no longer their prerogative and their prerogative alone. Grant Fox is exceptional but Simon Hodgkinson is right behind and launching a serious challenge. No big match could be more delicately poised or more important to the immediate futures of the champions of the Northern and Southern Hemispheres. In the English camp we feel we have peaked at exactly the right time – 1991. In another 18 months it is quite possible that over half of the Grand Slam side will no longer be playing international rugby. Everything has now been geared to the World Cup in the autumn. We have tremendous self-confidence and firmly believe that the best is yet to come. The backs played some outstanding rugby in the 1990 Championship and the pack was brilliant in the 1991 Championship. If we hit top form collectively in the World Cup there should be no stopping us.

Everything is in our favour for the New Zealand game. We have home advantage and we have not lost a single international at Twickenham for over 3 years. The last time we played New Zealand at Twickenham we beat them by 15 points to 9 in 1983. New Zealand will have to fly from the other side of the world with a major time difference and only seven days to recover before they play us. It is a distinct disadvantage for them to play the deciding match in the pool first. They would have much preferred to have started by playing their games against United States and Italy to give them a chance to acclimatise. They would then have faced England two and a half weeks after arriving and with two matches behind them.

Having said all that, it will still be incredibly difficult to beat New Zealand but the odds are marginally in our favour and I expect England to win. After the shattering defeats by Wales in 1989 and Scotland in 1990 to deprive us of the Championship each season, I can guarantee we will not be the slightest bit complacent against either Italy or America in the other two matches in our World Cup Pool. In the past England have not always been at their best when they have played against teams they were expected to beat convincingly. Nonetheless, I think it is inconceivable that we could lose to either America or Italy and furthermore I expect England to adopt the All Blacks approach to such matches, which is quite simply to win by the biggest score possible. It is a ruthless, unsympathetic and highly successful attitude.

As I have already mentioned in passing, the winners of Pool 1 meet the runners-up of Pool 4. If everything goes according to plan then I anticipate England will play Fiji in the quarter-final at Lille. France have improved throughout 1991 and by the time of the World Cup should be just as formidable a side as they were at the last World Cup in 1987 when they reached the final before losing to New Zealand.

France have a few excellent new forwards who could well be a major force come October. They have a good new prop in Lascubé, a potentially top class lock in Olivier Roumat and some very exciting new loose forwards in Blond, Deslandes, Benazzi and Cabannes. They have a wealth of experience in such established internationals as Camberabero at fly-half and Mesnel and Sella in the centre. The French have two blisteringly fast and elusive wings – Lafond and Lagisquet and, of course, at full-back, Serge Blanco, the most capped player in world rugby. This will be his final month of international rugby before he retires so I expect him to enhance his enviable reputation with a dramatic final flourish.

This reshaped French side under new coaches Daniel Dubroca and Jean Trillo seems to have just about everything but I have a hunch they may lack the overwhelming power and strength of the English and All Black forwards although they may be a shade faster round the pitch and may have slightly better runners and passers up front. By any standards, France look sure to be one of the best sides in the autumn.

Indeed, I would be very surprised if they fail to beat Fiji fairly comfortably. Fiji have looked superb at the Cathay Pacific Hongkong Bank Sevens in Hong Kong for the last two years beating New Zealand in the spectacular final on each occasion but they are never as good or as committed at 15-a-side rugby. On that basis France should win Pool 4 with Fiji finishing as runners-up. Both should beat a Romanian side in the process of rebuilding and also Canada, although if there is to be a surprise in this section it is likely to come from the Canadians. They did remarkably well at the Hong Kong Sevens in March beating Argentina and the full national Scotland side and could have a very useful 15-a-side team in October.

Pool 2 looks a straight shoot out between Scotland and Ireland. They meet in the pool decider at Murrayfield after they have both played Japan and Zimbabwe who are most unlikely to pose either of the big guns any problems. In November last year all the serious money would have been on Scotland. They had won a Grand Slam, run the All Blacks close in New Zealand and put 49 points including nine tries on Argentina at Murrayfield. Ireland, on the other hand, had struggled desperately to beat Argentina in injury time at Lansdowne Road at the end of October and looked a long way behind Scotland. But they improved match by match in 1991, drew with Wales, pushed England all the way in Dublin and were considered very unlucky to lose to Scotland in their final match of the season.

That particular match was a dress rehearsal for the World Cup clash, although it has to be said that Brian Smith's decision to switch to Rugby League is a major blow to Ireland. Smith had some very good matches for Ireland and he will be hard to replace in the short time available. Ireland have a lively new pack with a good line-out expert in Neil Francis and some new promising backs like Staples, Saunders and, in particular, Simon Geoghegan on the wing. Centre Brendan Mullin is the ideal experienced player to hold the team together but they lack a recognised goal-kicker especially without Brian Smith and they have to travel to Murrayfield for their crucial deciding pool game.

Add to these disadvantages for Ireland the fact that the Scots have a settled, established side, a long unbeaten home record in internationals, two solid goal-kickers – Gavin Hastings and Craig Chalmers – and the fantastic coaching expertise of Ian McGeechan and I would fancy Scotland to finish top of Pool 2 with Ireland as runners-up.

Now it's time for Will Carling and his team to concentrate on the World Cup.

Wade Dooley believes England can win the World Cup, Roger Uttley prays he is right.

That would give Scotland a probable home tie in the quarter-finals against Wales which the Scots would be expected to win. Curiously enough, Ireland, as runners-up, would also enjoy a home tie in the quarter-finals against Australia in Dublin. Pool 3 looks clear cut in one way but a trifle vague in another. Australia look 20 points better than the other three countries and they should finish top. The big question is whether or not on current form Wales will finish in second place. They face two potentially hard matches against Western Samoa and Argentina. Both these challenges could grow during the summer and they could give Wales a real fright in October. Wales are suffering at the moment from their worst-ever record – they have gone eight matches in the Five Nations Championship without a win. They have chopped and changed their team all year and they are going through a very demoralising time at present – Western Samoa and Argentina are each capable of springing a surprise but I think Wales will re-group over the summer and bounce back to make their mark in the 1991 World Cup even though they are most unlikely to repeat their heroics of 1987 when they finished third.

Australia are an exceptionally strong well-balanced side with experienced players in the key positions – Nick Farr-Jones and Michael Lynagh are wonderful half-backs, there is the tremendous skill of David Campese on the wing, two fast, forthright centres and a pack full of power and pace. And, don't forget, Australia can boast they are the only side to have beaten New Zealand in the past five years. I don't think there will be a lot to choose between England, New Zealand, France and Australia. I have a hunch Scotland will be the best of the rest.

If my guesswork is right then this is how the four pools will look after the first ten days of the tournament.

Pool One	Pool Two	Pool Three	Pool Four
1. ENGLAND	1. SCOTLAND	1. AUSTRALIA	1. FRANCE
2. NEW ZEALAND	2. IRELAND	2 WALES	2. FIJI
3. U.S.A.	3. JAPAN	3. W SAMOA	3. CANADA
4. ITALY	4. ZIMBABWE	4. ARGENTINA	4. ROMANIA

The quarter-finals would then read as follows:

SCOTLAND v WALES
at Murrayfield
FRANCE v NEW ZEALAND
at Parc de Princes
AUSTRALIA v IRELAND
at Lansdowne Road
ENGLAND v FIJI
at Lille

If this does indeed turn out to be the quarter-final line-up, then I would feel fairly confident in predicting that the semi-finals will look like this:

SCOTLAND V NEW ZEALAND
at Murrayfield
ENGLAND V AUSTRALIA
at Lansdowne Road

That would, according to my crystal ball, lead to a 3rd place play-off match on the last Wednesday of October between Scotland and Australia and the final of the 1991 World Cup on the first Saturday of November would be a repeat of the opening match at the beginning of October:

ENGLAND V NEW ZEALAND
at Twickenham

Checking back to my forecast earlier in this chapter it seems we won that particular match so perhaps it would not be too wildly optimistic to hope for exactly the same result just four weeks later. Or does all this prognostication involve a dash of wishful thinking?

Cathay Pacific. The Airline for a world where gentlemen occasionally forget their manners.

Wherever gentlemen gather to
compete, play can become rather
intense. Particularly when the
game is business. So when you fly
off to do battle, choose the airline
that best understands the needs of
international business travellers.
Cathay Pacific. We'll ensure you
arrive in better shape to cover your
ears, save your face and triumph.

CATHAY PACIFIC
Arrive in better shape.